Making It Happen

BY Charles Paul Conn
The New Johnny Cash
Hooked on a Good Thing (with Sammy Hall)
No Easy Game (with Terry Bradshaw)
Just Off Chicken Street (with Floyd McClung)
Believe! (with Richard M. DeVos)
The Magnificent Three (with Nicky Cruz)
Julian Carroll of Kentucky
The Possible Dream
The Winner's Circle
Kathy (with Barbara Miller)
Making It Happen

Making It Happen

A Christian Looks at Money, Competition and Success

Charles Paul Conn

Fleming H. Revell Company
Old Tappan, New Jersey

Unless otherwise identified scripture quotations in this volume are from the King James Version of the Bible.

Scripture quotations identified RSV are from the Revised Standard Version of the Bible, copyrighted 1946, 1952, © 1971 and 1973.

Scripture quotations identified PHILLIPS are from THE NEW TESTAMENT IN MODERN ENGLISH (Revised Edition), translated by J. B. Phillips. © J. B. Phillips 1958, 1960, 1972. Used by permission of Macmillan Publishing Co., Inc.

Scripture quotations identified NIV are from HOLY BIBLE New International Version, copyright ©, New York International Bible Society, 1978. Used by permission.

Library of Congress Cataloging in Publication Data

Conn, Charles Paul.
  Making it happen.

  1. Success.   I. Title.
BJ1611.2.C66   248.4   81–7383
  ISBN 0–8007–1252–8   AACR2

TO RICHARD M. DEVOS,
who has taught me so much about so many things.
I admire him as a man,
respect him as a Christian disciple,
and love him as a friend.

Contents

Making It Happen

1
Bred to Run

The message of this book is that you and I were designed by the Creator for lives of richness and challenge. We were made for achievement and fulfillment. It was not intended that our lives be

boring
or constantly frustrating
or dominated by failure.

We were made for reaching and stretching. We were designed with the physical and emotional equipment to be constantly in a state of change and improvement. Everything about the way God put us together indicates an almost limitless capacity for variety and positive growth.

The pieces are there, inside us all. The energy is there; it is a part of being alive and being God's child. The world is there for us to explore:

the music is there to be heard
the sights to be seen
the songs to be sung
the mountains to be climbed
the people to be loved
the flags to be waved
the good life to be lived.

It remains only for us to make it happen, to bring all the pieces together wherever we live. And that begins when we genuinely believe that God has, after all, intended us to live abundantly.

"I will praise thee," the great poet David exclaimed, "for I am fearfully and wonderfully made: marvellous are thy works ..." (Psalms 139:14). All of us know something of how David must have felt. Wonderfully made, indeed! We are all individual marvels, 4.124 billion walking miracles, moving around on the surface of the earth, each one of us specifically engineered for full, rich living.

God designed the human eye for richness. Your eyes are designed for the entire range of the world's sights, to see things large and small, near and far away, strange and familiar. Your eyes are designed to see a thousand shades of colors, from the brightest scarlet reds to the smooth and soothing blue greens. Your eyes were made to see

> the twinkle of lights on the Manhattan skyline
> sunset over the Grand Canyon
> the massive rush of water over Niagara Falls.

Your eyes have the capacity to take in all that and more. You have great visual range: the ability to look at a tiny amoeba through a microscope; to see planets millions of miles away; or to see even more beautiful things, like

> the smiles of friends
> and the multicolored lights of a Christmas tree
> or your name on a diploma.

God doesn't expect you to settle for less than that!

What a waste to use our eyes solely on the dull grays of a black and white world, never seeing the color, the richness, the great kaleidoscope of the brilliant world we live in!

God designed our ears for great things, too. We were made to hear the great music of the world, to follow the intricate phrasings of a Bach prelude or a Chet Atkins guitar solo, to be overpowered by the thunder of Beethoven, to enjoy the rhythms of rock

and jazz
and gospel music
and country-western
and whatever else sounds good to us.

God made the ears with the capacity for it all: to catch the faint scrape of a violin bow as it pulls lightly across the strings or to absorb the battering of the loudest Fourth of July firecrackers. It's all there for our ears to take in, all those sounds that make an "ordinary" life a wonderfully extraordinary one.

Your ears! Those ugly-looking flaps of wrinkled skin that the Creator seems to have pasted so haphazardly on either side of your head! Just think what joy they bring into your life! They bring the sound of applause that's meant for you

> and the whisper in the dark—"I love you"—that's more beautiful than all the symphonies written
> and the squeals of your children as they open gifts on Christmas morning
> and the bleating of the gym buzzer that tells you the game is over and your team has won.

No person's ears were made for less than that.

Surely the God who gave us the capacity to hear so many wonderful things would not wish us to settle for the monotones of life, to accept a flat, featureless world, when there is such an explosion of joyful noise out there to be heard.

God designed our taste buds to sample a hundred cuisines. He gave us the ability to distinguish the sweet from the sour

> the spicy from the bland
> the crunchy from the slithery stuff.

We have the capacity for hundreds of acquired tastes—thousands, even. Using every type of vegetable and fruit and fish and bird one can imagine, the chefs and recipe writers of the world have given us an endless smorgasbord, with all sorts of tastes, including lasagna

    corn on the cob
    boiled eel from Holland
    bamboo shoots from Taipei
    homemade ice cream, just name your flavor
    a dozen subtle wine sauces
    and escargot (snails, if you please)
    hot Mexican tamales
    cold cucumber soup
    and Kentucky Fried Chicken, Extra Crispy or Original
        Recipe!

It's all out there, ready to massage our taste buds. The Creator gave us the range to taste it all—to love it or reject it, but to taste it and experience it. With the equipment He gave us for such wide-ranging pleasure, surely no one need settle for a life of hot dogs and hominy grits!

The human body is obviously made for rich, full experiences. Eyes, ears, muscles, nerve endings, brain, the senses of smell and taste: the design of all these physical systems reminds us that our bodies are made for creative, adventurous living.

Likewise, so are our emotions. We are designed to feel a mind-boggling assortment of feelings, so many we don't even have enough psychological terms to label them all. Each one of us, even the simplest, least interesting personality among us, is a creature of enormous emotional complexity. We are capable of such incredible feelings

    of such passionate desires
    of driving, relentless hungers
    of terrible, paralyzing fear
    and such aggravating laziness.

And then at times we surprise ourselves at the unexpected emotions that float to the surface:

the warm, good feelings when we pray
    the simple love for a child

an unexpected act of generosity
honest pride when we do something right
or that happy-tired relief when a tough job is finished.

Emotionally we are designed for richness. The Creator made ordinary people with an almost unbelievable capacity for emotional range. He gives it to all of us, however "average" or uninteresting our lives may seem to the people around us. Within that few cubic feet of protoplasm called *you* is an awesome potential for breathless, soaring excitement

for sturdy loyalties
for unselfish love
for being a friend and having a friend
for sharing: weeping when others weep
and rejoicing when others rejoice.

You were made to feel all those emotions. You were made to experience everything: the peaks and the valleys; the times of euphoria and the times of reflection; the mellow, laid-back moments and the eager, anxious ones; the laughter and the tears. You were made for full, rich expressions of the entire emotional range.

We owe it to ourselves, and to the God who made us, to utilize the full potential of what it means to be human. We owe it to ourselves to live life

not to back away from it
but to walk up to it and embrace it and enjoy it.

Too many people back away. Too many sell out short. They settle for less of life than they really want

less than they deserve
certainly less than God intends them to have.

Life for them becomes at best a comfortable rut, at worst a drudgery—long stretches of boredom interrupted by occasional periods of pain.

You don't have to live that way! "Life is not meant to be a

prison in which man awaits his execution," President John Kennedy once wrote. God never intended it to be that. He created man in His image, this magnificent piece of equipment into which He breathed His own life. He made us for happiness and achievement and a thousand good things. He gave each one of us an individual, unique stamp. No two are alike. Each one of us is a custom-built, one-of-a-kind model. Each one is equipped for a lifetime of loving deeply

> striving greatly
> and living well.

There hangs on the wall of my son's bedroom a picture of a young thoroughbred colt. The colt is only a few days old, and he stands in the awkward, gangling fashion of any newborn horse. He is mostly knobby knees and long, spindly legs with a body perched on top. Despite the fact that he is still a colt, barely able to stand and walk, it is obvious that he is a thoroughbred, a racehorse; already visible in his skinny frame are the signs of the champion he will one day become. The painting has a simple title that says it all: *Bred to Run.*

That awkward colt may be barely able to walk today, but somewhere in his genes are all the qualities of speed and strength, and in time they will emerge. He is bred to run, and run he will! He is the product of generations of lightning-fast horses. He is designed for the racetrack. Speed has been bred into him; when the time comes for him to run, he will stretch those legs, and the speed will be there.

We are all like that colt. We are bred to run, built for achievement, designed for success. It is our bloodline, a part of our heritage and our birthright. God did not design us for failure and unhappiness. He didn't intend us to be broken-down old nags and plodders. We, too, are bred to run! And we, too, begin as awkward and stumbling colts, not quite sure of ourselves, feeling a long, long way from the racetrack and the winner's circle. But the Master's design is there; and in time, if we give it a chance, it will show.

2

The Positive Power of Childhood

Of the many figures of scripture that describe the relationship between God and His human creatures, one particular analogy dominates the list: It is the view of God as Father and of us as His children.

This particular view of God and man recurs constantly throughout the Bible, in both Old and New Testaments. It is as if God, as He speaks to us in His Word, keeps returning to this metaphor, almost as if He can find no better, no truer way to describe our relationship.

Before we are "soldiers of the cross"
before we are "laborers in the vineyards"
before we are any of those things

we are the children of our Heavenly Father—plain and simple. We are His sons and daughters. He relates to us and loves us in much the same fashion that we relate to our own children and love them.

That is such a simple and rudimentary truth that many people slide right past it in search of something more elaborate. The attitude of a parent toward his little child is so universally understood, so easily conceptualized, that we hesitate to accept it as the ultimate model of God's posture toward us. It is so familiar, this love of the parent for the child. Merely a mention of it evokes immediate mental images: the loving father, eager to see the child enjoy life

21

eager to see the child grow
proud of the child's successes
taking delight in the child's well-being
willing to work long hours and make great sacrifices to
    provide good things for the child.

There is almost no limit to the father's willingness to *do* for
the child—not merely to love him in a passive way, but to *do*
for him.

That is the picture which God uses to tell us how He feels
about us!

It seems too good to be true—to think that

the great God Almighty
the Old Testament Jehovah
He of the thunderbolts and the terrible swift sword

looks down at me, and when He sees me, feels all the impulses
of love and tenderness that I feel when I look down at my own
small child.

That is difficult to accept when the God we heard about in
Sunday school was nine parts wrath to one part mercy. All
those visions from childhood of an angry, powerful God, easily
outraged and quick to punish—those visions are still too alive
down deep inside to let us immediately accept this fatherly
God. Having grown up with such an intimidating vision of
God, we are reluctant to trust this gentler version. *Is it really
true,* we wonder, *that God's attitude toward us is best illustrated
by our own attitude as parents toward our own children? Can that
view of God be trusted, or is it merely wishful thinking?*

Jesus answered that question, quite directly, in the Sermon
on the Mount: "What man of you," He asked His disciples, "if
his son asks him for bread, will give him a stone? Or if he asks
for a fish, will give him a serpent? If you then, who are evil,
know how to give good gifts to your children, how much more
will *your* Father who is in heaven give good things to those
who ask him!" (Matthew 7:9–11 RSV, *italics mine*).

That is an outright challenge to take seriously the parallel between our parental instincts and God's attitude toward us.

Does God want you to prosper?

Does He care about your success in secular pursuits?

Is it important to Him that you be happy, in the fullest and best sense of that word?

Does God want you to achieve all you can; will He help you make good things happen in your life?

The Matthew text is a good starting place for the answers to those questions. Jesus often taught, as He does here in the Sermon on the Mount, by asking questions. His disciples asked a question, and Jesus answered with a question of His own that showed them the truth. Our questions about success might also be answered that way:

Does it matter to you that your own child achieve and excel?

Do you want to see that child succeed in school or sports or music?

Do you take pleasure in his happiness?

Even in those areas of their lives that do not directly involve you, does it please you to see your children earn the rewards of their own hard work?

Of course it does! And so, also, with our Heavenly Father, we can be confident that He wishes the best for us—not just in spiritual matters, but in every part of our lives. "If you . . . know how to give good gifts to your children, how much more will your Father who is in heaven give good things to those who ask Him!"

There are limits, of course, to God's willingness for us to have whatever we want. It would be unreasonable to claim that God applauds every goal we set, that He always looks on approvingly as we charge toward those things we want. God does not want for us everything we want for ourselves, just as we do not want for our children everything their hearts are set on. It would be an indulgent and foolish father who would take such an uncritical approach to his children's pursuits.

We have all seen examples of such parental pushovers and understand that they generally produce spoiled and unhappy children. We recognize that it is no favor to a child to indiscriminately satisfy all his wishes. And so does our Heavenly Father.

I once heard a Christian say, speaking of a personal goal in his life, "God knows how badly I want this, and I know He wants me to be happy, so it must be His will for me to have it." That is not a reasonable conclusion—certainly not if we use the Matthew text as our guide—but it frequently appears, directly or indirectly, in the attitudes of high-achieving, ambitious Christians.

God may have very good reasons for withholding certain things from us

  things we greatly desire
  things for which we have worked hard
  things we think we absolutely can't live without.

Part of being God's child is accepting that. It goes with the territory. We are His children, and as surely as that brings good gifts from Him, it also requires bowing to His better judgment about things. The important point is that the outcomes, ultimately, are always good. *Always.*

Even in secular matters—God is our Heavenly Father even in secular matters. The areas of our lives that seem totally nonspiritual are important to Him, too. Some people have trouble believing that. They have God locked up in the church

  pasted up on the stained-glass window
  maybe chained to a pew somehow,

so that He is master of what goes on inside the sanctuary, but is uninterested in whatever goes on outside.

We have no difficulty believing that God cares about

the sins we commit
the tithes and offerings we pay
the church we attend
the prayers we pray
the scripture we read or neglect to read.

We all agree that He cares about *those* things. He keeps an eye on those areas. But does it really matter to Him about the other stuff, the ordinary, run-of-the-mill stuff?

Does God care if you get that promotion?

Catch that plane?
Make that sale?
Or if the interest rates go up too fast for you to buy that new house you've set your heart on?

Does He really care if you make a *B* instead of a *C?*

Or if you hit the ball out-of-bounds off the tee?
Or if the dinner gets done before the guests arrive?
Or whether your hair looks good tonight?

Does it matter to Him whether you make a little money or a lot of money, whether you win first prize or second, whether you get a date to the senior prom? Is God—the one, true, only, all-powerful Jehovah God—really so fatherly that He cares about such trivial matters in the lives of ordinary people?

Yes! Emphatically, absolutely, miraculously, the answer is yes!

It does matter. Not just the supernatural things, but the natural things matter to Him.

Jesus cared about such things. He cared whether His mother's friend had enough wine for her wedding guests. Cared so much, in fact, that He *did* something about it. He made more wine. Nothing particularly spiritual about that. In some ways, turning water to wine was the most revealing miracle He ever performed, because it demonstrated that His

interest and concern extend beyond the forgiving of sin and the
healing of disease. The little things mattered to Jesus.

> It mattered that His disciples were seasick and scared to
> death, so He calmed the storm.
> It mattered that the people who came to see Him became
> hungry; so He manufactured food, right on the spot.
> It mattered that His friends Martha and Mary grieved
> over the death of their brother. Mattered so much, in
> fact, that He wept right along with them, even though
> He undoubtedly knew that in a few minutes their
> grief would be ended. Jesus wept with them, because
> their grief mattered to Him.

The foundation of success—any success—is the knowledge
that we matter to God. We are His children, and He wants
good things for us, even to the point of becoming actively involved in the everyday affairs of our lives.

In life's little daily challenges, God is not neutral; He is actively on your side. He is on your side in those constant battles
with the blahs

> and the family budget
> and the crabgrass in the lawn
> and that smoking habit you can't seem to whip
> and the bad plumbing upstairs
> and all those things that get you down.

He cares.

He cares because you are His child.

If you let Him, He will help you make things happen—good,
positive things—every day of your life.

3
The Aristocracy of Excellence

A few years ago, I attended the commencement exercises of a small high school in Michigan. The valedictorian of the class was honored that night, and in her speech, she said something that made me hurt for her, so poignant were her words. "First of all," she said to her classmates, as she accepted the award, "I don't want anyone here to think I feel that I'm better than any-one else." Here she was, at the crowning moment of twelve years of work, feeling obliged to apologize for her academic su-periority.

Somehow I recoiled from her apology. I wanted to interrupt her right there, to affirm the meaning of her accomplishment. I felt like standing up in the gym and shouting to her, "Don't apologize for your achievement! Don't be reluctant to accept the credit for what you have achieved!

> Admit it!
> Embrace it!
> It is your right!
> You have earned it!
> Enjoy this moment; you have worked hard for it and you deserve it!"

Most of us can identify with that girl, because in one way or another we have been there. We have felt that subtle pressure to apologize for our successes in the classroom or on the job or in the community or even in our own families. We have had that vague sense that superiority is like a wart on the face, to be hidden from others, lest they be offended by it. We are expected to shrug off accomplishments and say, "Aw, I was lucky," or, "Aw, it was nothing," lest someone think we take ourselves too seriously.

It is important not to succumb to that pressure. People who work hard to reach personal goals *are better persons* than they were before, because they persisted, and they worked, and they *made* it. Nobody gave it to them. There is nothing wrong with striving to be "better." When you finish a tough job, you are a better person—not before God, of course, or in any absolute sense—but you *are* nevertheless better than you would be had you quit because you didn't care about achievement. You are better than if you had never started, because you had no vision or no ambition. You are better than if you had been unwilling to pay the price to succeed. *Most* important, you are better than *you yourself* were when you began. Because of your effort and vision, you are better!

That is not a popular idea. It never has been. It is basically the idea that some have called the *aristocracy of achievement:* the idea that people can elevate themselves by hard work, and that when they do, they are entitled to the rewards of their extra effort.

Many people don't like to talk about aristocracy or even to hear about it. It is a subject that seems almost contrary to the American experience. Aristocracy, strictly defined, is a government by the best individuals, by a privileged class. More broadly an aristocracy is a layer of individuals, the top level in any society.

In earlier days the aristocracy of Europe, and indeed of this country, was an aristocracy of birth. One was a member of the aristocracy because of his last name, because of the genetic pool from which he was drawn. The American experience swept away that aristocracy. For 200 years in this country we have said that one man is not better than another by birth, that the American aristocracy should not be based on bloodlines. In the place of that old aristocracy, we erected a new one, an aristocracy based not on an accident of birth or the color of skin, but based on personal achievement, on excellence of performance.

That aristocracy is a source of enormous vitality in American life. It is God's great gift to each one of us. And that aristocracy still exists. It exists in every town

on every campus
in every corporation
in every community
every profession.

The strength of the American experience is not that we have swept away *all* aristocracy, but that the aristocracy which we recognize is one that any one of us, by sheer strength of will, can enter.

There is a line from the novel *Ragtime,* which, describing a particular character, says: "He did not believe in aristocracy except that of the individual effort and vision." That line perfectly captures the challenge that we all face: to believe in no aristocracy but one of individual effort and vision. Americans refuse the notion that any individual is better than another because of the cut of his clothes or the sound of his name or the place of his birth.

But the greatest hazard in the 1980s is not that of believing in a false and superficial aristocracy, but that of believing in none at all. Somehow, by some perverse logic, there is a sentiment that argues that there should be no aristocracy at all, that all men are created equal and should remain always equal in every way, that somehow for an individual to seek to be *better* than the crowd is

undemocratic
unchristian
unseemly
and just downright neurotic!

That was the pressure the high-school valedictorian felt that night—the pressure to fall back to the level of the crowd, to blend in, to embrace a standard lower than the one she was personally willing to meet.

That pressure has always existed. It operates in every group of people, whenever someone dares to reach out to become better than the herd.

> "Cut him down to size!"
>
> "Whaddya think you are—better than everybody else around here?"
>
> "Look at him!" one man says to another as a mutual friend walks across stage to receive an award. "He really thinks he's *somebody!*"

We must be prepared to resist that pressure and go on believing in an aristocracy of excellence. It is important not just to believe in being better, but to be *hungry* to be better.

With what, then, will we compare ourselves? If we want to be better, the question is, "Better than what?" And the answer is always, "To be better than yourself." There is no fuel that will power our lives—outside the love of God Himself—more forcefully than the hunger to be better today than we were yesterday.

The English novelist George Eliot once said, "We can never give up longing and wishing while we are thoroughly alive. There are certain things we feel to be beautiful and good, and we must *hunger* after them." What do you feel to be beautiful and good? In your own private moments of dreaming and wishing, what can you see yourself achieving?

> Whatever it is
> however impossible it seems
> whatever the obstacle that lies between you and it
> if it is noble
> if it is consistent with God's Kingdom, you must hunger after it, and stretch yourself to reach it.

The Rubber-Band Principle

The great challenge for all of us is to stretch. We were engineered to meet challenges. God made us to stretch. God created man something on the order of a rubber band. A rubber band is made to stretch. When it is not being stretched, it is small and relaxed; but as long as it remains in that shape, it is not doing what it was made to do. When it stretches, it is enlarged; it becomes tense and dynamic, and it does what it was made to do. God created *you* to stretch. He did not intend you to be always relaxed, always to maintain your present shape. It is when you are stretching that you are living up to your own promise. It is only by stretching that you become better.

The temptation of course is to compare ourselves with those around us, and we cannot afford to do that. You cannot afford to compare yourself with any other person, observe that you are in some way achieving more than that person, and be pleased with yourself. The question is not, "Are you better than someone else?" The question is, "Are you stretching? Are you reaching?"

If you can make *B*'s without stretching, you must make *A*'s. If you can finish second without stretching, you must finish first.

If you can do one job without stretching, you must do two.

Any goal that you reach without stretching is set too low, and reaching it is no achievement at all, however much other people may applaud you for it or may even covet it for themselves. *You* know what you are capable of. *You* know when you are stretching. And it is *you* whose evaluation matters.

Constant stretching keeps us from spending too much time comparing ourselves only to each other. Most of us swim in a rather small pond in a very big world. In his poignant novel *The Wayward Bus,* John Steinbeck offers this description: "One night a week he played poker with men so exactly like himself that the game was fairly even, and from this fact his group was convinced that they were very fine poker players."

Doesn't that sound familiar? There will be groups like that everywhere you turn, all sitting in small circles, turned in toward one another, congratulating one another on life's narrow, petty victories, never daring to look over their shoulders at the wider, richer world around them. Theirs is a conspiracy of mediocrity. "You refuse to strive," they say to one another, "and so will I."

Whenever we find that spirit, we must refuse to lend ourselves to it.

We must never be ashamed of wanting more.
We must never be embarrassed by our hunger.
We must never believe that to strive for a better world, or
    a better life, is somehow an act of disloyalty to the old one.
We must always be willing to be hungry—hungry to
    sing a better song

      write a better letter
        bowl a higher score
          make a bigger profit
            set a better example
              give more support to the causes and people
                and organizations we believe in.

When we are no longer hungry for that, we lose something precious. When we quit stretching, we quit growing; we quit living.

People use many excuses to avoid this stretching, growing process, because it necessarily produces internal tension and sometimes even a certain kind of alienation.

The rubber band is more relaxed, perhaps more comfortable, when it is not being stretched. But it is also unproductive. To be constantly striving *does* produce tension. It does indeed have its discomforts. It can be frightening to be out there where you've never been before, trying to do something you're not quite sure you can do; but that is what stretching involves.

How many times lately have you been scared by the audacity of what you were trying to do? How recently have you been involved in a project that made you wonder if you weren't perhaps out of your depth? Have you ever felt like an imposter, just to be *trying* to do what you were trying to do? If not, maybe you haven't been setting your goals high enough, maybe you haven't been really stretching.

The aristocracy of accomplishment is not a relaxing life, but if we are to grow, we must be willing to live with the tension and accept the ordinary stresses that go along with it as a normal part of life.

Some people avoid stretching, not to avoid the tension, but because they have listened to the popular lie that says mediocrity is somehow conducive to spirituality, that somehow it makes a man more spiritually sensitive to be technically sloppy.

That is a spiritual cop-out, pure and unadorned.

How is it possible that an individual, by slovenly habits and lack of skill, could thereby bring himself closer to the heart of God? That is an insult to God. It is told that an old man once arose to denounce John Wesley after he had preached a particularly scholarly sermon. "Young man," he shouted, "God can't save the world through your education." "No," Wesley replied, "but he can do more with my education than he can with your ignorance."

God has always used technical skills to achieve spiritual purposes. Martin Luther translated the New Testament into German, not out of his ignorance, not out of some mysterious, divinely concocted, miraculously acquired blessing, but out of a highly refined excellence in the Greek and Latin languages, which he acquired through sweat and toil and effort. How many of us have worshiped and been moved spiritually by Handel's "Hallelujah Chorus"? That work of music didn't spring full-blown from the mind of a lazy but highly spiritual Christian. It came from a man who had learned how to write a score, stack a chord, orchestrate a melody.

When we stretch, we give God more to work with, and He honors that stretching if it is for His Kingdom and in His

Name. God will not save the world through our achievements, but He cannot save it through our laziness either.

To the extent that we are willing to reach past our comfortable limits toward true excellence, we can expect God to meet us with His enabling power. He sees our attempts to become more than we have been before, and as a Heavenly Father He can only lend Himself to our efforts.

4

But What of the Failures?

By now you may be beginning to feel that all this "happy talk" simply doesn't square with the facts as you know them. "It sounds good," you say. "But does it mean anything?"

A reasonable question. Words are cheap, after all; they are good for very little, unless they mean something. No naked person ever dressed in words; no freezing man ever warmed his hands by them; they are poor substitutes for a roof overhead; and though they are said to be eaten from time to time, certainly they have no nutritional value.

It all *sounds* good, you say, to talk about the fantastic human equipment we have and how we are designed for greatness and how God is our Father and He wants us to prosper and live abundantly. But how does that square with the fact that so many people are

> frustrated
> broke
> unhappy
> bored half to death
> and generally miserable?

"If life is a bowl of cherries," Erma Bombeck asks, "what am I doing in the pits?"

We all ask that question at one time or another. "Spare me the happy talk, mister, and tell me where I can get a job." It is a gap that won't go away, the gap between the ideal and the actual, the potential and the here and now. Up to now, we have been talking about life as it can be, but there is for most of us a long distance between that and life as it is. The questions are there and call for answers:

> If I am made for success, why do I fail?
> If I am meant to achieve, why am I so often a loser?
> If God wants me to be fulfilled, why am I so empty?
> If I am born the child of the King, why do I feel so worthless?

All the positive thinking in the world,

> all the speeches
> all the books
> all the slogans and posters on the wall
> all the heartwarming stories

cannot obscure the reality of human failure. It is there. There are many negative realities in our world, and they cannot be ignored or explained away. Nor should they be.

Death is real.

So are cancer and air pollution and the rising murder rates

> in Detroit
> Los Angeles
> and New York.

Fatal automobile accidents are real. So are birth defects and oil prices and venereal disease and income tax. You can't talk those things away or sing them away or exercise such prodigious powers of positive thinking that they disappear or even shrink a little.

> There they are.
> They are bad.
> They cause pain.

There is nothing positive to be said about them. The best that can be done is to identify the problems about which we can do something and do something about them. The rest we chalk up to individual human failure or the caprice of nature or to the intrinsic flaws of this or that social system. But the important thing is that we do not allow their presence to diminish our joy in the rest of life, the truly good and beautiful things in life. It is important to believe that over the long haul, in any individual life, the good will always outweigh the bad if we are willing to work for it and fight for it.

For example: We have all heard of greedy doctors and incompetent ones. Malpractice suits are practically a national joke. But we don't close down the medical schools and give up on the entire profession.

It was recently reported that a thirty-eight-year-old man checked himself into a metropolitan hospital in New York complaining of stomach pains. The physician on duty diagnosed the problem as an abdominal tumor and suggested surgery to remove the tumor. The surgery began. Oops! No tumor. Misdiagnosis. Instead the surgeon found over 500 metal objects in the patient's stomach, including:

300 coins
a can opener
parts of knives, forks, and spoons
a key chain with keys
and a broken thermometer.

That's a rather badly misdiagnosed stomach tumor.

Such stories leave us shaking our heads, but by no means do they tempt us to reject modern medicine itself. Even the fellow with the junkyard in his stomach no doubt headed straight for a doctor's office the next time he was sick. He has to figure nobody's perfect, so the doctor blew the diagnosis. But that's no reason to give up on the medical community entirely.

That quite sane approach is taken in respect to the flaws that constantly appear in government

and education
and the court system

and the airline industry
and the predictions of TV weathermen.

Things are never perfect, but we don't give up believing in them. All these systems are potentially capable of being perfected, we reason, so we go on working with them and trying to use what we know about them to make them better.

An example is traffic fatalities. Automobile accidents are a fact of life in America. Almost 25,000 people are killed by them every year. Surely no intelligent person believes that a year will ever pass when no one is killed on America's highways. We realize that traffic deaths are an ugly reality we must always live with. And yet....

And yet we work hard to achieve that unreachable goal. We spend millions of dollars; we employ thousands of people.

> We lower the speed limits
> We increase police patrols on holidays
> We put up billboards and run safe-driving ads on television and radio and in the newspapers
> We teach driver education in the schools
> We test safer automobiles
> We build concrete buffers in the medians and put reflectorized signs on the roadside and cut grooves in the pavement to improve traction
> We put Saint Christopher on our dashboards and say prayers as we leave on long trips and tell our friends to drive carefully almost by reflex.

And still the deaths continue, just as we know they will. The important point is that we don't quit trying. We don't give up on the problem. We don't let the terrible negative numbers overwhelm us. Though we realize we will fail in the big goal of ending highway death, we refuse to give up.

It is our modern version of dreaming the impossible dream, fighting the unbeatable foe. No reasonable person would argue with making the effort. Tens of thousands of us are alive today who would be dead otherwise. We do what we can, and though we never are satisfied, we never quit trying, and we all are infinitely better off for it.

The struggle of an individual to take charge of his own life

to succeed in his business or profession
to reach whatever personal goals matter to him
to achieve something
to win
to break through
to feel good about himself:

Those are battles worth fighting, too! Those are dreams worth believing in, however faraway their total and perfect realization may be and however many examples of failure litter the path. It is moving toward that goal that counts; it is the will to push ahead that makes life better.

Positive thinkers sometimes take a bum rap.

They are accused of being unrealistic

naive
Pollyannaish
deluded into believing in the perfectability of that most
imperfectable of all creatures, the human being.

And the skeptics hurl into the argument, as ammunition, the evidence of individual failure.

They miss the whole point.

They do not understand that progress is made by the accumulation of many partial successes. The very act of trying to become something better than what one already is, even if temporarily unrewarded, lays the groundwork for future advancement.

The point is that we believe our effort does matter

that we can be better
that life is not mad and chaotic
that striving will eventually pay off.

"If we wait until we do things so well no one can find fault with them," a great minister once said, "we will never get around to doing anything at all."

5

The Key to Achievement

People who achieve great things are all alike.

Not in ways that show, of course. Physically there is no way to tell the winners from the losers, the champs from the chumps. Big achievers come in every imaginable physical package. They come from

> every part of the country
> every race and culture
> from all sorts of families
> from big towns, little towns, no towns at all.

Winners may be healthy or handicapped

> young or old
> strong, strapping, athletic-looking men
> or little old ladies with varicose veins.

Still, in the things that matter, people who achieve great things are all alike.

I have known lots of winners. Knowing them has been a gift to me from my profession, an unexpected result of being a professional writer who spends his time writing about the heroics of other people. I have known many people who have achieved greatly, and it has been my job to talk with them

> and hang around and watch
> and find out why they are winners.

What I have learned is that they are all alike. A diverse collection of them comes to mind immediately: an all-pro football player (6′ 3″, 220 pounds, he eats Big Macs in three bites), a corporate president (middle-aged, sophisticated, wealthy), an Arizona teenager (attractive, blonde, courageous), a big-time entertainer whose name and face are known around the world, a Dutchman who smuggles Bibles, the governor of a Southern state, an intense young gangfighter-turned-evangelist, and so on.

They have demonstrated their greatness in different arenas:

> in the marketplace
> at the ballot box
> on the football field
> before the stage lights
> or facing Idi Amin's army.

But the qualities that make them extraordinary people are strikingly similar. What they are on the inside is as *similar* as their jobs and hometowns and physical appearances are *different*. The same few building blocks of great achievement appear in every conceivable human activity.

Theodore H. White, a contemporary journalist and historian, has interviewed virtually every internationally prominent person of our generation. Stalin, Churchill, Roosevelt, Hitler, de Gaulle, Kennedy, Mao Tse-Tung, Nixon, Ghandi, Pope John, Douglas MacArthur—the list goes on and on. For over forty years he met them all, and he concludes that they share common qualities which made them great and powerful men, whether for good or ill. Chief among those qualities, White says, is that their minds reject defeat and that they have the desire to impose their wills on events.

My own experience with great achievers is much less impressive than White's, but my conclusion is the same. Here is my list of the qualities shared in common by great men and women:

1. *They choose their own goals and are undaunted by criticism from unfriendly sources.*

Gore Vidal, the great American novelist, was viciously criticized in the early years of his career. He was a young writer, still not established in his craft, and reviewers savaged his first books. Years later, after Vidal was successful and famous, an interviewer from *The New York Times* asked how he had survived those early years of rejection and criticism.

"I survived," Vidal answered, "by understanding that it is *I* who am keeping score!"

Winners keep their own scorecards. They decide on a correct path and follow it. The voices they hear and follow belong only to God and their own inner spirits. They understand that the most plentiful commodity on earth is free advice, usually critical advice, often hostile and uninformed advice. The achiever is by nature somewhat isolated from the less visionary people around him. He almost always has a different view of what is possible in life, of what is worth going after. He hears the "different drummer" of Thoreau's famous metaphor.

Rich DeVos, one of the nation's top business leaders, says it this way: "It is always the fellow who has never made ten thousand a year who knows all the reasons why you can't make fifteen. It is always the tenderfoot who recites the reasons that you can't make Eagle Scout. It is the college flunk-out who can explain why you're too dumb to get that degree, the fellow who never ran a business who can best describe the obstacles that make it impossible for you to get started, the girl who never entered a golf tournament who can tell you why you don't have a chance to win. Don't listen to them. If you have a dream, whatever it is, dare to believe it and try it. Give it a chance to happen! Don't let your brother-in-law or your plumber or your husband's fishing buddy or the guy in the next office rob you of that faith in yourself that makes things happen. If you have that flame of a dream down inside you somewhere, thank God for it, and do something about it. But don't let anyone else blow it out!"

The election of Jimmy Carter to the United States presidency in 1976 was one of the most dramatic up-from-nothing victories in modern political history. When he began running for the office, he was openly laughed at and derided. The newspapers in his hometown of Atlanta poked fun at his apparently futile fantasy. Even his own mother, when he announced to her, "Mother, I'm going to run for president!" is said to have laughed and responded, "Well, for heaven's sake, president of *what?*" But none of that mattered to Carter. Only his own inner voices mattered. One year before the election, less than 2 percent of American voters had ever heard of him. A national poll rated the top eleven candidates, and he was so obscure that his name wasn't even included among the eleven. He opened his campaign in Des Moines, Iowa, with a reception in a downtown hotel, and only two people showed up. Ten months later, he was President of the United States.

Achievement of great goals must always occur in the face of misunderstanding and often outright criticism. Albert Einstein was once urged to quit school because he was judged by his teacher to be not quite bright. He became one of the greatest scientists in mankind's history. Winston Churchill was disgraced by the failures of British naval policy during World War I and was so devastated by critics that he was generally thought to be finished as a career politician. But he came back, at the age of sixty-six, to become Prime Minister of England and carve his mark as one of the greatest leaders of this century.

2. *True winners never accept any temporary failure as a final defeat.*

Great men and women fail. No doubt about that. Almost every biography of great leaders is pockmarked with accounts of failure. Great generals lose battles. Great politicians lose elections. Great athletes lose games, even championships, sometimes even their jobs. But the common qualities they share are a refusal to quit when failure comes, the unwillingness to accept defeat, the determination to fight back from reversals and misfortune.

Abraham Lincoln, perhaps America's greatest president, lost more times than he won. He failed in business in 1831, was defeated for the legislature in 1832, again failed in business in 1833, then was elected to the legislature in 1834. But in 1838 he ran for Speaker and lost; in 1840 he ran for Elector and lost; in 1843 he ran for Congress and lost. Oh, well. He tried it again in 1846 and was elected, but was defeated and lost his job in 1848. In 1855 he ran for the Senate and lost. In 1856 he tried for vice-president and lost again. In 1858, perhaps thinking his luck had changed, he ran a second time for the Senate. He lost again. But in 1860, only two years later, he ran for and was elected President of the United States!

Now that is a pretty dismal record if you're adding up all the defeats. But who's counting? The race that counted was the last one, the big one, the one in 1860. It gave him the opportunity to become one of America's greatest leaders and the president who saved the Union. Ask any school kid who Abraham Lincoln was, and you'll hear nothing about

> all those defeats
> all those failures
> all those lost elections
> and embarrassing rejections.

You'll hear about what matters: That he was a great man who, over a hundred years later, still enjoys the gratitude of his nation.

Terry Bradshaw is widely acknowledged as the premier quarterback in professional football. It wasn't always that way. After a good start early in his career with the Pittsburgh Steelers, his performance began to deteriorate. The worse he

played, the harder he pressed, and that only made it worse still.
He fumbled

> and threw interceptions
> and called the wrong plays
> and made just about every mistake a quarterback can
> make, except one: He didn't quit.

He lost his starting job and was moved to the second team,
then to the third team. He wondered if he would ever throw the
ball for the Steelers again. He got hurt, and the hometown fans
cheered the injury. They didn't cheer the player—they hadn't
cheered him in weeks—but cheered the injury! It was the
lowest point in a season studded with low points. But he didn't
quit.

That was seven years ago, and today he is at the absolute
peak of his game, the only quarterback in history to win four
Super Bowls, and winner of the league's most valuable player
award. People who haven't followed Bradshaw's career closely
may think old number twelve has always been on top. No way.
He knows more about how it feels to lose than most people
ever learn. But he refused to accept the defeats as permanent.
He shrugged them off, battled through them, and finally the
good times came. That's the way it always is with great
achievers.

3. *Truly successful people are willing to do the things that
others are unwilling to do.*
Small things often add up to big accomplishments. Usually
they are the unpleasant things, the inconvenient things, the
things that seem at the time to have little to do with the overall
success of an enterprise.

The late Vince Lombardi, one of pro football's greatest
coaches, said it best: "Winning is not a sometime thing: it is an
all-time thing. You don't win once in a while. You don't do
things right once in a while; you do them right all the time."
Lombardi's teams won championships because he convinced
them to do all the little things

    the unglamorous things
    the sweaty, inconvenient things
    the things losers neglect to do.

Lombardi understood that those were the small things that add up to big victories, big accomplishments.

I worked with a politician once, in the state of Kentucky. He was something of a political phenomenon, a golden boy. He seemed to have a magic wand that he waved to make things go right. His victory margins in statewide races set all-time records. He was elected governor by landslide votes never seen before in that state.

I asked Governor Julian Carroll once what was the secret of his political magic. He answered without a moment's hesitation: "Well, Paul, I've always been willing to do the things the other guys weren't willing to do!"

The records show that it is true. He did the inconvenient things. The glamorous things are no problem; anyone will do those things. It's not hard to find people who will speak at the big rallies, with TV cameras and thousands of the faithful on hand to grin and applaud.

But it's tough to do the little potluck dinners
in the little backwoods towns
with the little crowds
and the long sleepy drive home through the mountains

    from Dawson Springs
    and Wallonia
    and Paintsville
    and all those other little places that only God and the
        Jaycees and a truly extraordinary politician seem to
        know about.

That's when record-breaking political victories are won— years before election day, when an ambitious young legislator is willing to meet the people and shake the hands that will one day mark the ballots.

Have you noticed how some people seem always to be lucky, always to get a break just when it matters most, and how many times those are the same people who are willing to do the little things, the inconvenient things that add up to achievement? Such luck is created by hard work; it is not simply found by the side of the road, as it seems to be.

"Luck," says baseball coach Branch Rickey, "is the residue of design and desire."

Whenever I hear of a successful person's "big break," I look for the trail of small sacrifices that led him to it. Luck almost always works that way. I have a brother who is a successful contractor. He has built a thriving construction business at a very early age. I have heard him called "lucky," more than a few times, because so many things have turned out so well for him. But when I hear that word applied to him, I think of all the things he does that other men in his position will not do, and of all the years he has been doing them.

When a truck needs to be driven,
    he drives it
When a blueprint needs to be delivered,
    he delivers it
When push comes to shove and the work goes past midnight,
    he doesn't flinch.

When the little jobs are there to be done, he has always done them, for as long as I can remember. And he has always managed to be in the right place at the right time. That's what Branch Rickey was talking about: Luck is the residue of design and desire.

People who achieve greatly all seem to have that kind of luck.

6
The Power of Believing

God makes no mistakes.

He never has.

Sometime, long ago, back when nothing existed but Him, He designed a master plan for the world we live in. When He was at the drawing board, He did everything perfectly: nothing left out, no wasted material. By the time He got to Genesis 1:1 and began bringing into existence this big universe and our little planet Earth, the shape and makeup and component parts of every living thing were designed.

God gave to every created being the specific thing it most needs to function best. Every creature's most important function is matched perfectly with a component part that is naturally the most impressive component of that particular creature.

The bird, for example, is made to fly. Flying is what birds are all about. Birds *invented* flying; flying is their most important activity.

So what is the principle feature of a bird's makeup? Wings, of course! God matched the most important function with a perfectly developed means of executing that function: a wing! All sorts of wings, in fact. For the hummingbird, who flies very fast and hovers and floats in the air, there are small lightweight wings that can beat hundreds of times per minute. For the sea gull, who likes to float and cruise on the ocean winds, there are large, wide wings, wings that catch the currents like giant sails and allow the gull to glide, barely moving his wings, to cover the long distances he travels. To the ostrich, who is so big and strong that he hardly needs to fly and really prefers to walk or run anyway—at up to forty miles per hour—God gave barely any wings at all. The ostrich has stubby little wings, just enough to let everyone know he's a bird.

Form follows function. If a bird's most important activity is flying, then a bird's most highly developed feature is his wings.

And so on—fish swim, so they have strong, well-developed tails and fins, not to mention gills with which to pull oxygen from the water. Tigers eat the flesh of other animals, which must be caught and killed. So look at those teeth and claws (and don't ever try to outrun one!).

It is a reliable pattern. Every creature is given a highly developed component part that corresponds to its most important function.

What about man? What is his most distinctive function? What is most important about man? Our highest and most important function is to interact with God, to worship God and give Him glory, to communicate with God and respond to Him. Man's most important activity is his spiritual activity. That is his distinctive feature; that is what makes man, man. Just as fish were created to swim, as surely as

> birds were made to fly
> snakes, to crawl
> antelope, to run
> cattle, to graze,

just so surely was man made to interact with God, to know Him, to love and be loved by Him.

So it follows naturally that God's design is to give man his greatest ability in the area of his most important function. He made us to know Him; and to know Him we must have a spiritual component, a part of us that is built for seeing what the eyes cannot see, for accepting what the mind cannot comprehend. So He gave it to us. He gave us the power to believe! The best-designed, most highly developed part of man is his spiritual component, the thing inside him that makes faith possible.

What wings are to the bird and fins to the fish, so is the power of faith to man!

The power of believing. The power of faith. It is the most impressive part of man, the most highly developed, the source of our greatest energy. God gave us superb physical equipment; He gave us brains like computers

> eyes that can see many miles
> muscles that can lift heavy weights
> skin that repairs itself
> a heart that pumps blood thousands of times an hour, day after day, for dozens of years, without missing a single beat.

God gave us lots of impressive equipment, but skin and bones and tissue and glands and muscles are not what man is all about. Lower animals have all those things. What makes man unique is the ability to believe, to have faith, to see the unseen; and that power to believe is man's most powerful property. It is the best and brightest part of man.

So when you hear about the power of believing

> or the "magic" of believing,
> or the "miracle" of believing
> or such phrases as that, don't dismiss it too quickly as just so much talk, just so much rhetoric from the positive-thinking preachers.

The power to believe is much more than a catchphrase, more than just words from one of those success-and-motivation books. It is as real as—and much more important than—hair and skin and arms and legs and the other parts of man that are visible.

God gave man the power to believe so that man could know Him and worship Him. The ability to believe was made for spiritual activity, but it is not confined to that. When God gave us the wherewithal to believe, He made possible the exercise of faith, not just toward Him, but toward other things as well. Our faith can reach out in other directions as well as toward God—and quite appropriately so. It is part of being human, part of being made in God's image, to be able to believe not only in God, but in ourselves

>in other people
>in causes and movements
>or in the future and what it holds for us.

When true faith is present, it generates the energy that makes things happen. That's no myth. That's no old wives' tale. It's more than just wishful thinking. Things really *do* begin to happen when one believes strongly enough.

As more is learned about the human body and the way it works, it is increasingly apparent that what was once thought to be a clear-cut division between the body and the mind is not so clear after all. Psychologists are finding more and more evidence of the power of the mind to change things physically, to produce measurable, visible change within the body. A book by Norman Cousins in 1980 sent shock waves through the intellectual community, because of its bold assertions about the power of the mind. Cousins is not a psychologist; he is a former editor of *Saturday Review* magazine and one of the most respected thinkers in the country. His book, titled *Anatomy of an Illness*, describes his own successful fight against a crippling disease by using laughter and happy thoughts and talk. It was a therapy that worked.

That sounds absurd and simpleminded.

It sounds too good to be true.

It sounds like the kind of thing you hear around the office during coffee break; you forget it immediately because you feel the case couldn't possibly be that simple.

But it *is* that simple. It is a well-documented, intelligently argued example of the power of thinking to produce recovery from an illness when drugs and other conventional medical therapies were inadequate. The power of believing is more than just wishful thinking; it is a source of energy in the human system. It makes things happen.

This medical case and other recent findings similar to it do not surprise those who seriously understand faith as an energy source in human affairs. Great achievements—in secular as well as religious pursuits—have always been made by men and women of faith. People of vision, people able to see what is possible rather than what is actual, people willing to commit themselves to something that is not yet visible—such people have been the shakers and movers in every age of human history. It is the "true believers" who have built the big corporations

>made the important discoveries
>explored the new territories
>won the critical military victories
>led the powerful movements
>invented the new technologies
>found the medical cures
>and written new athletic records.

They can, who *believe* they can!

Virtually every great achievement is made after someone dares first to believe it can and will occur, usually in the face of the skepticism and disbelief of others. The United States put men on the moon in 1969—and beat the Soviets at it—because the right people believed we could do it and do it first. Out of that faith came the goal and the commitment to the goal and then followed the work, the sacrifice, the struggle, and finally the victory. But first came the belief.

Great achievement almost always follows that pattern. Faith is the catalyst. It is the trigger. It is the first and most basic part of the process.

If you were asked to name the elements of success, your list would probably be a rather predictable one. All the books and tapes and speeches about success talk about the same things; they stress the importance of

    having a dream
    setting a goal
    a healthy self-concept
    persistence
    hard work
    refusing to quit

and all those other familiar elements of success. All those elements rest on the foundation of simple faith. Believing is the underpinning of every one. None of it—goal setting, hard work, persistence—will operate in the absence of simple belief that good things *can* happen as a result of it all. Believing is the basic and most necessary of all the components of success. Without it, none of the rest happens.

The power of believing *does* have limits, of course.

Faith alone is not always sufficient to change things. In fact, it rarely is. Unless that faith is followed by action, it rarely changes anything at all. And even then, there are times when all the faith in the world won't change things. The power of believing does have certain limits. If it is raining buckets of water, walking out the door and shouting "I *believe* the sun is shining!" will not keep the believer from being drenched, however much he believes it. He will merely be both wet and foolish.

Positive thinking has gotten a bad name in some quarters because some people claim too much for it. Believing has two important constraints within which it must operate. Gung-ho positive thinkers sometimes forget them. Here they are:

First, believing must be based on facts.

Second, believing must be followed by action.

Belief Based on Fact

Let's look at the first of these constraints: Belief must be based on facts, on an accurate premise. In other words, what one believes must square with things as they are or *can be*. To believe truly in a myth, or a lie, or a foolish notion

however fervently
and sincerely
and totally and tenaciously the person believes in it,

still adds up in the end to foolishness. It is not noble to believe in a blatantly untrue premise; it is idiocy, plain and simple.

A housewife can scream "I believe I'm a butterfly!" all day long, and when the day is over she is still not going to be a butterfly. She will merely be a very hoarse housewife.

The problem, of course, is that the premise is faulty. A woman cannot become a butterfly—period. It is not within the range of possibility. All the belief in the world and all the affirmation in the world are absolutely wasted if the premise is faulty. The upshot of that rather obvious principle is that it matters *what* one believes. Some people fail to understand that; they feel that believing, in itself, is the only thing that matters—that one can believe in anything and bring it to pass.

What emerges in such cases is a slogan that says, in effect, "What one believes to be true, *is* true." As beguiling as that sounds, it is unfortunately wrong.

When I was a child, I knew a man in my hometown, who believed he could carry on conversations with trees. He sincerely believed it. He could be seen along the sidewalk, earnestly chatting with a big sugar maple about who-knows-what-all. He believed the trees talked back to him. He believed they were his friends. He was psychotic, of course. We don't put a guy like that in the Believers' Hall of Fame; we put him in an institution. Lack of sincerity or lack of belief was not his problem. His problem was that what he believed was not based on facts.

The need for accurately based beliefs challenges us to base our belief in ourselves on the premise that we are the children of a personal and loving God. That is the only true and sturdy base for belief in oneself. It puts the individual in the position of believing in himself because God believes in him. He loves himself because God loves him. He is confident about his future because he is God's child.

On the other hand, belief in oneself that is based purely on one's own talents

> or ambition
> or energy
> or personal competence

builds on a shaky premise. When belief in oneself is based sheerly on one's own strength, on some purely humanistic confidence in the perfectability of man, that person somewhat resembles the housewife who believes herself to be a butterfly. Man, all alone, without any help, is not usually a match for the big, bad, cruel world—not over the long run.

There is a solid basis for belief in oneself, one's abilities, and one's future. It is found in Philippians 4:13 (*italics mine*): "I can do all things *through Christ which strengtheneth me.*" That is the base from which all true self-confidence proceeds. It is the most powerful form of belief in oneself, because it is based on facts, and that is important. It is important *what* one believes and *why* he believes in himself, not merely that he does so.

Belief Followed by Action

The second important constraint on the power of believing is that it must be followed by action.

Belief is the catalyst for positive change in one's life, but the change usually occurs not as a direct result of the belief itself, but as a result of the behavior which the belief produces. Because we believe, we are willing to *do* things, to commit ourselves to a plan of action. It is that action which brings the results. Few of the miracles that are accomplished by faith are accomplished by faith alone, but by the persistent, hopeful labor that the faith produces.

This principle is consistent with scripture. The Apostle James said it clearly: "Faith, if it hath not works, is dead." This man is telling us that there are some things that require one's own action and work. Simply believing is not good enough.

It is for this reason that the power of believing is best applied to those areas which respond to our own involvement, areas in which the believer and his efforts are the critical variable. Faith is most effective in situations when *you* make the difference, because faith makes the difference in *you.*

That is the problem with the man who decides to believe it is sunny when in fact it is raining. The sun and the rain do not depend on him; the weather does not respond to him; it has nothing to do with him. Believing has little chance of bearing on that particular situation. Only an outright miracle can change the weather.

The power of believing is strongest, on the other hand, when there is direct contact between the individual and the problem at hand. The weather doesn't respond to human effort, but most other things do, and believing operates powerfully in those cases.

If the areas of your life that frustrate you include such matters as where you work

> where you live
> how much money you make
> what kind of friends you have
> how well you perform
> what you contribute
> how much influence you have

or a thousand other areas of life, the power of believing can make an enormous difference in what the future holds.

Not because the pieces will fall magically into place.

Not without effort and hard work.

But because once you believe you can, you will!

7
Making It Happen

When simply believing is not enough to get from where you are to where you want to be, what do you do next?

There are several reliable principles that help along the way. They are explained in different ways and tagged with different labels, and most of them start with simple common sense. The best thing that can be said for these principles is that achievers generally observe them and nonachievers generally do not.

Principle of Massed Attack

The assistant principal of my high school was a sturdy, nononsense woman named Mrs. Clemmer—"Inez," behind her back. She gave me a bit of advice one day; she singled me out for it personally, in fact, and it stuck like a dart.

"Never forget, young man," she lectured sternly, jabbing her glasses in my direction, "that no matter how much you have to work with, it's never going to be enough if you spread it too thin."

Touché.

I was one of those kids who tried to dabble in everything. I rushed from one activity to another and never did any of it as well as I could have or should have.

Winners concentrate their energies. They are willing to eliminate low-priority activities from their lives and bring all their talents to bear on the few things they decide to be important.

That principle is best illustrated in the military arena, where small armies often beat large ones by skillfully massing their strength at critically important times and places. Field Marshal Erwin Rommel, the brilliant German general of World War II who was called the Desert Fox, was once asked what single strategic principle contributed most to military success. His response: "Concentrate your force at the point of attack."

The battle is not to the largest army, but to the one whose forces can be brought to the point of attack. It doesn't really matter how many soldiers are in uniform if they are spread out over a thousand-mile front. The tightly concentrated striking force will punch through the thinly stretched defense every time.

No one has enough talent to do everything well. Those who achieve greatly understand this early in life, select one area of interest, and commit all their personal resources to that one grand obsession. That requires a certain sacrifice, but in the end the payoffs are usually worth the price. If there is a specific goal that really matters, the first priority must be to discard other interests which siphon off time and energy and emotional resources from that one goal. The winner decides what he wants to attack, then he masses his forces at that point. That type of single-mindedness accompanies almost every great achievement.

All of us have seen those athletes who play fairly well all the time, but never seem able to have that one great, emotional effort when it counts. This is another form of dissipated effort, the net result of which is that the individual never wins a big victory. The world is full of those who play well in practice, sing well in rehearsal, shoot holes in one when no one is watching, bowl scores of 300 when it doesn't count. The winner is the one who performs best when it matters most. He muscles up for the big ones.

The thing that separates winners from losers is often not that the winner has more ability more desire

more energy

or certainly not that he has more hours in the day.

What he has is a tighter focus. He has a trimmer, more stream-lined personal agenda, with fewer dangling, low-priority activities. Those goals that he sets receive a larger share of his own resources. His forces are concentrated at the point of attack, and that's how the breakthrough occurs.

Why are so few people willing to organize their lives in this way? Why are we so reluctant to observe such an obvious principle? Probably because to do so means that some things must go. Some activities, some claims on our time, even some that are themselves quite positive and good, must be eliminated in favor of a massed attack on the items of highest priority. It can be painful to do that. The process requires lots of second-guessing, sometimes serious soul-searching

deciding who you really are

and what you really want

and what things are most important.

That's not an easy process, and consequently we avoid it. By stretching ourselves thinly over everything, we avoid the tough decisions about what things in life we really love most. We keep all our options open, and in the process never reach our full potential in anything.

To maximize any single part of our lives, something has to go.

I have a friend in British Columbia who illustrates this point well by describing the mental anguish he suffered when he cut down trees on his building lot to make room for his house. He had grown up as a boy on the flat, treeless prairies of Alberta. Things there were brown and dry. When he moved to Vancouver, he selected a suburban lot with large, beautiful trees. To fit the house on that lot, some of the trees had to go. He was determined to avoid that, so he altered the house plans, drew dozens of sketches, turning the plans this way and that. Nothing worked. It was clear that for that particular house to go on that particular lot, some of the trees had to go. It really didn't matter how pretty they were; they had to go to make room for the house.

It is so with our lives. To do a few things well, other things have to go. Hitler couldn't win a war on three fronts, and neither can we. Our force must be concentrated at the point of attack.

Principle of Inclusion

One of the best-kept secrets in life is that including other people in one's goals lends energy and impetus to reaching the goals themselves. The old stereotype of the lonely, solitary striver, grasping for recognition and achievement without regard for anyone else, is actually a rare case.

The truth is that people who achieve greatly usually *share* greatly.

A successful friend of mine, a skillful attorney, first showed me this time-honored principle. "There are basically two kinds of people in this world," he said. "Two kinds, the *ex*cluders and the *in*cluders. Some people live to get everything they can for themselves and keep it for themselves. They exclude as many people as they can, because they think that will leave more of the goodies for themselves. Then there are people I call includers. They include other people in everything they do. They share their whole lives, including the rewards, with other people. And the funny thing about it is that they seem always to have more left for themselves than the excluders do. The more they share, the more they are able to keep."

Sharing is so basic to the human experience that the person who forgets how to do it loses more than he gains. Have you ever noticed how many of the successful people you know are the ones who enjoy including others in what they do, sharing life with them, giving away with one hand what they work so hard to acquire with the other? Think of the most successful people in the conventional career categories of the high-achieving

> teachers
> entertainers
> businessmen
> athletes
> ministers
> physicians
> and you-name-it.

Look at their success in any of those professions, and it probably will involve the desire and attempt to include other people in some way.

The really good *teachers* are those who have a compulsion to share what they know with their students, not just to teach the subject matter. The good geology professor is more interested in his students than in geology. His commitment is to them and not to the rocks! He is a good teacher because he wants to share. He is not content merely to learn all he can about geology, but wants to *include* as many students as he can in that knowledge and love for his field.

The most successful performers and entertainers are those who reach across the footlights and share themselves with their audiences. Their concern is not just with the music—singing the notes right—or with the script—saying the lines right. The pedestrian performers can all do that. Even mediocre singers can sing the notes. No, that is not what makes a good entertainer truly brilliant. The legendary performers have been those who pull their audiences right into the middle of what they are doing. They share with the audience; they *include* everyone in the concert hall in what they are doing.

The truly great athletes are the ones who include their teammates in their achievements. The really good physicians are those whose major concern is with the patient. The most in-

fluential ministers are those whose primary interest is to share
the message with as many people as possible, to include more
and more people in what they are doing.

This principle holds even in the world of business, which has
the image of a rough-and-tumble arena where supposedly the
operating rules are

> dog-eat-dog
> every man for himself
> survival of the fittest
> law of the jungle
> get yours first and let the other guy worry about himself.

Even in the world of business, the successful entrepreneur is
usually someone who has a product he genuinely believes in
and wants to share with the public. Sure, he wants to make a
profit, but he also has a sense that everyone needs what he has.
The best insurance salesman is always the one who has an
evangelistic zeal to see as many people as possible with wall-
to-wall coverage. He sells more insurance because his attitude
is one of sharing, of including others in a good thing, not of
merely dumping a policy, picking up the check, and heading
for the nearest exit.

Big achievers are big includers. Somehow the act of sharing
what they have achieved, of including others in it, gives the
achievement itself more meaning. It validates the importance
of having worked so hard for it in the first place and gives the
energy and urgency to go out and achieve still more.

The Picture-Window Principle

The Picture-Window Principle is the concept that striving is
easiest when you keep the big view in sight. Looking through a
peephole is no way to stay motivated when you're moving toward a goal.

The big view is important. It takes big dreams

>   big goals
>   big rewards
>   big faith

to keep us moving through obstacles and fatigue and discouragement. To maintain momentum requires constantly reminding ourselves what we are working toward.

Achievement so often occurs in small, progressive steps that it is easy for the dream to be lost in the shuffle. Nothing will stall the march toward a goal quite so quickly as forgetting the thing one is working toward in the first place. It takes lots of practice putts to make a pro golfer, lots of those sleepy mid-morning lecture sessions to get a Ph.D., lots of deposits in the Friendly Neighborhood Savings and Loan to save the money for that new house, lots of late nights at the office to earn a promotion and a raise in pay. But most of us will stick it out and do all the little, tedious things, so long as we remember what it all adds up to in the end.

The problem comes when we get so wrapped up in the little problems along the way that we forget the big picture.

The best—or worst—example I know of losing sight of the overall view was the crash of an Eastern Airlines jumbo jet in the Everglades of Florida. The plane was the now-famous Flight 401, bound from New York to Miami with a heavy load of holiday passengers. As the plane approached the Miami airport for its landing, a light that indicates proper deployment of the landing gear failed to come on. The plane flew in a large, looping circle over the swamps of the Everglades while the cockpit crew checked to see if the gear actually had not deployed, or if instead the bulb in the signal light was defective.

When the flight engineer tried to remove the light bulb, it wouldn't budge, and the other members of the crew tried to help him. As they struggled with the bulb, no one noticed that the aircraft was losing altitude, and the plane simply flew right into the swamp. Dozens of people were killed in the crash.

While an experienced crew of high-priced pilots fiddled with a seventy-five-cent light bulb, the entire plane and its passengers flew right into the ground! That may be the ultimate example of allowing a small detail to divert attention from the bigger picture.

With less tragic results, many people lose sight of the larger context in which the day-to-day grind finds meaning. Highly specialized types of labor have increased our detachment from the end result of our work in so many ways that we become accustomed to it. We understand that the rivet we bolt into a piece of metal will someday, in some other production plant, be part of a sleek new automobile; but we personally never see it, so we lose sight of it. The rivet is a rivet is a rivet. It is there, just something we see all the time, and we quit trying to relate to it as part of a larger, more meaningful whole.

That's unavoidable for that nine-to-five factory job. Do the job and get paid, and that's the end of it. One learns to get his fulfillment and satisfaction from other parts of his life. When the task is a voluntary one—when the job at hand is not a matter of punching the clock and making a wage, but is rather a self-initiated effort to do something beyond the nine-to-five routine—well, then the ability to see the end from the beginning becomes vital. In that situation, only a clear vision of what one is building, the end product for which one works, will fuel the effort required to keep going.

If that big picture is kept in view, even the most mundane activity can be meaningful and exciting. When the big picture is kept in view, you don't lay bricks, you build cathedrals; you don't loop pieces of yarn together, you knit sweaters; you aren't just memorizing vocabulary words, you're learning a new language; you aren't merely calling on a list of accounts, you're becoming a vice-president; you don't just teach Sunday-school lessons, you make disciples for God's Kingdom.

The big picture! Keep that view of the big picture!

I have never given birth to a baby. (I am, unfortunately, physiologically ill-equipped for the job.) But my wife has, three times. Each time, I have marveled at the way she shrugs off the inconveniences of being pregnant, how she copes with the tedium and discomfort of those nine months. All expectant mothers do that. They tolerate, usually quite cheerfully, several months of a highly inconvenient physical condition. Have you ever wondered what sees them through the pregnancy with their positive attitudes and sweet dispositions intact?

I think I know.

I believe it is their constant awareness of the end product! It is their natural and God-given tendency to keep the *big picture* in view! For those nine months, the mother lives with a visual image of that baby. She thinks about it

> she dresses it in frilly things
> she loves it
> she coos at it
> she wonders about its sex.

She already has plans for it, all before the baby is even made. The mother never thinks embryo. She never dwells on the intermediate stages of fetal development. Her stomach swells, and she thinks of the final product. For months before it finally happens, she is having a baby!

To reach big goals, to make significant accomplishments, we must similarly concentrate, throughout the process, on the glittering goal that draws us. That commitment to the big picture makes the entire effort more exciting and the final accomplishment more meaningful.

8
When God Says No

So far we have talked about a good God who wants good things for His children and well-motivated people who want to stretch and grow to earn the richness of life.

That seems like a perfect combination: individuals eager for the good life and a God who wants to give it to them.

Why then, does anyone ever fail? Assuming a willingness to work hard for life's rewards, why don't those rewards automatically come to everyone from the hand of the loving Heavenly Father?

In chapter two, we talked about the scriptural analogy of God the Father giving good things to us, much as an earthly father gives good things to his children. Even a good earthly father, who might be inclined to be something of a pushover from time to time, doesn't give the child what he wants every time. The loving response to a child's desires is not always an affirmative one.

However badly we may want certain things from life, and however willing God is for us to live richly and fully, a Christian cannot automatically expect to sail through life getting whatever his heart desires.

Consider these three situations in which a parent might say no to a child or when our Heavenly Father might not assist us in

achieving
or acquiring
or experiencing

those things that we have set as goals for ourselves.

1. *God may not help us reach our goals if they involve rebellion against Him or rejection of Him.*

Would you help your child run away from home? or give him the money to do something in direct defiance of your orders? Not likely. Nor is God likely to help us reach goals that constitute willful movement away from Him. However much He wants us to be happy, he wants us first of all to be His. When we rebel against Him and consciously violate His will for us as we know it, He can no longer be expected to help us get where we want to go.

Rebellion of this sort may take different forms. It may involve breaking God's moral code, breaking His law. Or it may be a more personal type of rebellion, an act of ours that involves disobedience of what we feel, in our hearts, God has called us to do. This is a highly subjective, intensely personal experience. No one can make a judgment in this area but the Christian disciple himself.

A biblical example of this type of rebellion is found in the story of Jonah. God told him to go to Nineveh to preach, and he flatly refused to go. He had other plans. It doesn't appear that he sinned or broke God's moral law in any flagrant way, except that he had a clear sense that God wanted him to do one thing, and he set out to do something else instead. So God, rather than facilitating his plans, frustrated them, and that's how he ultimately found himself in the belly of a whale.

There is no reason to believe that God has stopped interacting with people in this way. He still has specific things for specific people to do at specific times. When He does, that person will always know. He may regard it as a calling, or a divine inspiration to do a certain thing or some other private experience that may take a variety of forms. Only God and the person involved can know for sure. But when that sense of obeying God is there and we ignore it or rebel against it, God cannot then be expected to assist us as we go in our own direction.

2. *God may not help us reach our goals if we don't select them in consultation with Him.*

God expects us to submit our plans to Him. He wants us to talk to Him about them—not after the fact, but all along the way. As parents, we dislike having full-blown plans dropped into our laps, already neatly packaged and set in motion by our children. (Even less do we like to find out what our kids are doing *after* they've botched things for themselves.) We like to be consulted as they go along, and have opportunity for input as their plans and goals are developing.

So does God. Proverbs is scattered with expressions of the idea that God wants to be involved in the daily process, not just to have things announced to Him on rare occasions—like on Easter Sunday or when we're in big trouble! "In all thy ways acknowledge him, and he shall direct thy paths" (Proverbs 3:6). The word *acknowledge* is the interesting one in this familiar verse; it is such a gentle word, such a carefully chosen word to urge the child of God to allow God into his planning. God doesn't want to take over our lives

> to call the shots
> to jerk us into line and
> make us do everything in a particular way.

"Acknowledge him," the verse says. Just acknowledge Him; just give Him a chance to provide some direction.

And in another place, we read the same call for interaction with God at the goal-setting stage: "Commit to the Lord whatever you do, and your plans will succeed" (Proverbs 16:3 NIV).

Whatever you do. The Bible is clearly not talking just to preachers here. This is not talking about the high and lofty things of the church, the sacred things of the priesthood. This is

a call to the everyday believer, to the simplest child of God—
both a call and a promise

> to the businessman
> and the housewife-mother
> to the student in the library
> and the pharmacist with his bottles
> and the cabdriver
> and the salesman
> and the schoolteacher who feels like giving up.

To all of us it is both a challenge and a promise: "Commit it to
God, and He will help it to succeed."
    It is particularly interesting that this verse talks about *plans.*
It is the plans that God wants to take a look at.
Not the past.
Not the already-squandered days.
Not even the things that are now in progress.
    God wants us to commit the *plans* to Him—the *goals*—the
dreams—the thing out there in the future that draws you so
powerfully that you're willing to write it down on a piece of
paper and dream about it and work toward it. Those are the
things God will help to succeed.

    3. *God may not help us reach our goals if reaching them will
ultimately bring us pain.*
    As natural parents, we so often tell our children, "No," on
the basis of our superior wisdom that the catchphrase "father
knows best" has become part of the vocabulary. When all else
fails, when we are unable to talk our children out of something
we don't want them to have, we always resort to the old
standby: "No, son, I know you're too young to understand it,
but this wouldn't be good for you. I realize how badly you
want it, but I know what's best for you." We've all heard that
speech—or given it—a hundred times. But sometimes the parents' superior wisdom isn't superior at all. The parent, like the
child, is often just guessing, and he is often wrong.

That's not the case with God. He knows the end from the beginning. He knows every turn in the path

>every square inch of the landscape
>every nook and cranny of a great big world we are just beginning to discover.

This Father *does* know best—every time—and He wouldn't be a loving Father if He allowed us to have things He knows will be ultimately destructive.

Would you give your small child a loaded revolver to play with, or a sharp knife? Would you give your child a wolf for a playmate, even if the child found the wolf cute and cuddly and saw no danger? Of course not. And neither will God allow us things that will destroy us, if we commit our plans to Him. No matter how much we reach for them, He will protect us from our own mistakes.

There is another time God may say no to our goals, and that is when we are not yet ready for the thing we seek. Would you let your daughter start wearing a bra at the age of five, just because she wanted it? Would you let your son borrow the family car at the age of ten? or your children to go to grown-up movies when they're still in grade school? You would refuse them, and not because there is anything intrinsically wrong with those things themselves. You allow them all those things in due time. But you'll say no for now, because you know your child just isn't ready for them yet.

God's timing is always better than ours. He brings us along slowly and skillfully. We get impatient. We want it all now. Sometimes we set goals that may be good goals, worthy goals, but which we are not ready to handle. When we do, it only makes sense that a loving Father will keep those things out of our reach.

Only God knows what might be the implication for your overall well-being if you become famous

>or wealthy
>if you married that girl

got that promotion
cut that hit record
or simply could afford to move to that neighborhood
   you've always wanted to live in.

He knows.

And part of what it means to be God's children is to accept that He knows and that He will help bring what is really best into our lives—not what we want every time, but what is really best for us.

9

Where Are the Five-Talent People?

There is no record of when the urge toward self-improvement first appeared—probably with Adam and Eve. It seems always to have been around.

As long as there have been people, some of them have wanted to do things better one day than they did the day before. Someone has always wanted to run a faster mile

grow a tastier turnip
build a taller building
write a better book
make a larger profit
climb a higher mountain than he has ever done before. And sometimes more than *anyone* has ever done before.

Perhaps everyone desires upward mobility to some extent, but some people desire it more than others. These people seem to use certain words a great deal—words like *achievement* and *motivation*. They talk about *self-improvement* and *excellence*. They read books with words like *success* and *winning* in the titles, and use phrases like "getting ahead" or "a bigger slice of the pie." They often speak of goals and dreams and ambition.

People who talk of such things have always been around; but in the past several years, their number has swelled dramatically. More people are spending more time than ever before thinking and talking about these ideas. Self-improvement has virtually become a movement.

As any movement will, it has attracted critics.

Among those critics are some Christians who distrust the growing emphasis on the potential of the individual to make a better life for himself. They feel the overall environment created by the success-and-achievement ethic is basically alien to the Christian life, because of its emphasis on competition, material gain, and the attempt of the individual to address and solve his own problems.

"Is it really a good idea," they ask, "to tell people they can meet their own needs, when they should depend on God instead?"

"Is it consistent with Christian teachings," they ask, "to encourage competition and self-advancement, when the Bible teaches us to prefer our brother?"

"And what about all this talk of money and creature comforts?" they ask. "Shouldn't a true Christian be unconcerned with earthly concerns? Shouldn't he spend his time, instead, on spiritual things?"

These are not trivial questions: not for the individual who sincerely seeks God's purpose, but who finds himself drawn toward a life of secular achievement; not for the ambitious Christian who wants to work for the fullest, richest life he can have. The question of whether these values are compatible deserves a good, hard look.

Achievement for What?

Few people would argue that striving to achieve great things for the church or for God's Kingdom is a bad idea. It is proper
to work as hard as you can,
do as much as you can,
be as good as you can for the church, most would agree. But

achievement outside the church is to some a different matter; in strictly secular pursuits, an intense desire to achieve seems to them unspiritual.

Such an attitude issues from a simplistic and unscriptural view of God's Kingdom. It carves the world into two separate divisions: the spiritual and the secular. It says that people should have compartmentalized lives: Some things are spiritual and are to be done one way; other things are secular and follow a different set of rules.

To the Christian, though, no such sharply divided world exists. We do not have two lives, a spiritual one and a secular one. We have only a single, all-inclusive experience. We are—or should be—Christian in everything we do: whether the Christian is working at his church or on his job, whether singing in the choir or painting the house, whether studying the Bible or studying his professional journals. The Christian does it *all*—secular or spiritual—to the glory of God. And it follows logically that he operates, then, with all his energy and at his very highest level of skill. The Bible says it this way: "... whatsoever ye do, do all to the glory of God" (1 Corinthians 10:31), and this way: "*Whatever* your task is, put your whole heart and soul into it, as into work done for the Lord ..." (Colossians 3:23 PHILLIPS, *italics mine*).

God tells us to commit all we do to the Lord, then do it with all our might, doing it in His name and "as unto Him," or just as if it were for Him that we were doing it. If a particular activity is immoral or illicit, if it is done in rebellion against God, if it is something of which God disapproves, then the Christian should not do it at all, and the question of whether he does it well or poorly is an irrelevant one.

If we do something "to the glory of God," we glorify Him most when we do it best. In this world we are God's representatives; we are His ambassadors; other people judge God by what they see in us. In such a world, how could it possibly bring glory to God for His followers to be

lazy students
   careless employees
      irresponsible businessmen
         sloppy craftsmen,

in short, *failures* in whatever they do? How can God receive glory from that? God is best glorified by people who give life their all-out effort, people who are willing to work a bit harder, stay up a bit later, get up a bit earlier to achieve all that is within their potential.

Certainly that was the case in the Old Testament church. God laid down specific rules for how He was to be worshiped and glorified by the people. The rules called for worshipers to bring as offerings to the Lord the first fruits of their farms, the very best quality products of their labor. God required them to bring the *best* grain, the best corn, the best fruit, the best calves and sheep. God was not interested in the quantity of the gift so much as in its quality. He was glorified by one bushel of top-quality grain more than by two or five or ten bushels of second-rate stuff.

God wanted the best His people could produce.

He still does.

It is inconceivable that such a God would be displeased with disciples who set high goals and work hard to achieve them, whether those goals are academic, athletic, financial, or career ones. God is glorified by our successes more than by our failures. Our willingness to attempt great things, to maximize our opportunities to honor Him, brings Him more glory than for us to retreat from the challenges, afraid to risk ourselves for fear we might fail.

That is the principle illustrated by the parable of the five talents, one of the best-known stories Christ tells in the New Testament:

It is just like a man leaving home who called his household servants together before he went and handed his possessions over to them to manage. He gave one five thousand pounds, another two thousand and another one thousand—according to the man's ability. Then he went away.

The man who had received five thousand pounds went out at once and by doing business with this sum he made another five thousand. Similarly the man with two thousand pounds made another two thousand. But the man who had received one thousand pounds went off and dug a hole in the ground and hid his master's money.

Some years later the master of these servants arrived and went into the accounts with them. The one who had the five thousand pounds came in and brought him an additional five thousand with the words, "You gave me five thousand pounds, sir; look, I've increased it by another five thousand." "Well done!" said his master, "you're a sound, reliable servant. You've been trustworthy over a few things, now I'm going to put you in charge of many more. Come in and share your master's rejoicing." Then the servant who had received two thousand pounds came in and said, "You gave me two thousand pounds, sir; look, here's two thousand more that I've managed to make by it." "Well done!" said his master, "you're a sound, reliable servant. You've been trustworthy over a few things, now I'm going to put you in charge of many more. Come in and share your master's rejoicing."

Then the man who had received the one thousand pounds came in and said, "Sir, I always knew you were a hard man, reaping where you never sowed and collecting where you never laid out—so I was scared and I went off and hid your thousand pounds in the ground. Here is your money, intact."

"You're a wicked, lazy servant!" his master told him. "You say you knew that I reap where I never sowed and collect where I never laid out? Then you ought to have put my money in the bank, and when I came I should at any rate have received what belongs to me with interest. Take his thousand pounds away from him and give it to the man who now has ten thousand!" (For the man who has something will have more given to him and will have plenty. But as for the man who has nothing, even his "nothing" will be taken away.) "And throw this useless servant into the darkness outside, where there will be tears and bitter regret."

Matthew 25:14–30 PHILLIPS

Like the three servants, we are all given our share of talent, time, opportunity, ability—all the things that come to us unbidden from God's hand. Some are given more than others. All, however, are expected to make the most of what they are given

$$\left\{\begin{array}{l}\text{to use it}\\\text{to enlarge it}\\\text{to work with it}\\\text{to stretch it}\\\text{to make the most of it.}\end{array}\right.$$

That involves work and trying. It involves risk. It requires sticking out one's neck, swallowing hard, and *trying* something. The thing about the one-talent man that triggered the master's wrath was not that he was stubborn or rebellious or dishonest, but that he was so *afraid!* He was too afraid of failure to try something for his master. He didn't know for sure what was the safe thing to do with what the master gave him, so he did nothing at all!

There is no indication that the one-talent servant did not love the master. That servant seemed quite willing to cheerfully return his one talent. The problem was not with his dedication, but with his inaction.

How much do you love God? Enough to sing a hymn for

Him and attend a worship service for Him, surely. But do you love Him enough to practice the piano for Him?

> enough to lay a brick?
> enough to go back to night school?
> enough to lift weights?
> enough to move to a new job?
> enough to try a new business venture?
> enough to take the effort to make yourself into the best possible person, so that the you He has is a man or woman whose total life brings Him glory?

Two Critical *IF*s

This approach to Christ-glorifying achievement makes sense, however, only if two critical conditions are met: The first is that these quests be done for God's glory; the second, that God's other children not be abused in the process.

It is fairly apparent that not all personal achievement is done for God's glory. Many people choose to operate entirely outside any personal acknowledgment of God; others start toward a goal with God's glory in mind, but lose sight of Him along the way.

When I lived in Atlanta, several years ago, I noticed in the Yellow Pages, in the listing of restaurants, an entry for a place called Church of God Grill. The peculiar name aroused my curiosity and I dialed the number. A man answered with a cheery, "Hello! Church of God Grill!" I asked how his restaurant had been given such an unusual name, and he told me: "Well, we had a little mission down here, and we started selling chicken dinners after church on Sunday to help pay the bills. Well, people liked the chicken, and we did such a good business, that eventually we cut back on the church services. After a while we just closed down the church altogether and kept on serving the chicken dinners. We kept the name we started with, and that's Church of God Grill."

They started out selling chicken to support the church and somehow forgot about the church in the process. Only the chicken survived.

Lots of people do that. They start out to become great achievers for God's glory, and God's glory gets lost in the shuffle. The idea of striving for success, so that God will be honored, makes sense only if we stay in touch with God in the process. It can be done, and it very often is done; but it requires us to monitor our own hearts constantly to maintain a fresh dedication of our efforts to Him.

It also requires an ongoing sense of gratitude to God for the resources by which we achieve. One of the Christian's potential hazards concerning an emphasis on individual effort is that of forgetting who makes it all possible. The hardest-working, highest-achieving person alive still has plenty to be grateful for, and staying in a posture of gratitude to God helps to remind us that we do it all for His glory.

Even as we celebrate the human spirit—that magnificent energy that underlies all great success—we do so with gratitude to the Creator, who made it and put it deep within us.

A second *if:* Seeking success for God's glory makes sense only if we treat other people well along the way. There does seem to be something of a hierarchy of virtues in the Christian value system; and in such a lineup, behaving fairly toward one's brother gets a higher rating than personal achievement. When Jesus tells us that the two great commandments are, "Love God," and, "Love thy neighbor," He indicates the high priority He attaches to our interpersonal relationships.

Any accomplishment is tarnished for the Christian if it occurs at the expense of hurting others.

Some people have used this point as the basis for an attack on competition itself. Any form of competition, they argue, requires that there be losers as well as winners and is thus contrary to the spirit of Christian love. This view ignores the degree to which the competitive model is inextricably a part of basic human nature. It is as natural as breathing itself, and to argue against all forms of competition is logically insupportable. In some other world, perhaps. But in this life, in these bodies, with the human nature God has given us, certain forms of competition are inseparable from life itself.

The forms of competition that are unchristian are those in which the emphasis is on the humiliation of the loser or those in which one competitor cheats the other or takes unfair advantage of him. If in order to succeed, an individual feels compelled to put the other guy down, to destroy him, to treat him as an enemy to the point where he would make him suffer, that is competitive success at the cost of Christian love. That kind of success can hardly occur to the glory of God.

Despite the many prevalent images to the contrary, most highly successful people do *not* succeed at the expense of others. The principles of success work against the person who is ruthless and unfair. However many stories are told of those who climb to the top over the bodies of their victims, that is rarely the case. That behavior bears the seeds of its own failure. Most winners do not "win through intimidation" or by "looking out for number one," but through cooperation with others, plus lots of hard work and sacrifice.

Competition is not unchristian. A disciple of the Lord can compete without being any less a disciple; he can compete, and he can win. But he must acknowledge that there does exist a distinctly *un*christian competitive spirit, which is a hazard to be constantly avoided. Much of the contemporary emphasis on "winning" advocates a crassly selfish, mean-spirited approach to competition. Pleasure comes from beating others, rather than from achieving one's own best performance. Victory becomes the occasion for shouting over one's own success. That approach to competition is impossible to reconcile with the model of caring and considerate disciples.

The Christian competes because these are things he is hungry for, and he is willing to work hard for them—not because there are other people over whom he wishes to demonstrate his superiority.

Great accomplishments will always be more difficult than modest ones. It will always take extraordinary effort to achieve extraordinary things. Some choose the path of modest goals cheerfully and intelligently, casting no stones at their more ambitious neighbors. Others, unfortunately, seek to explain that the more successful neighbor must surely be less spiritually attuned than they. How else could he have risen so high, they cluck, except by forgetting God and taking advantage of people and chasing the things of the world?

That is a cop-out, plain and simple.

It ain't necessarily so.

There are in this country today—as there have always been—tens of thousands of sensitive children of God who are great achievers in every area of life.

> In politics and sports
> business and entertainment
> academics and civic affairs

they compete and win. They set high goals and accomplish them. They burn midnight oil. They push hard and care deeply and achieve greatly. They do it all without neglecting God and without abusing other people.

They are the five-talent people.

Their achievement brings honor to themselves and glory to God.

10

The Bible and the Dollar Bill

Nothing man has ever invented receives so much attention, is so widely discussed, generates so much controversy as this small item: It is a piece of paper measuring 2⅝ by 6⅛ inches with a thickness of .0043 inches. It takes 490 of them to weigh a pound.

It is the dollar bill.

Ah, yes, we know it well. Money: It is both used and abused, worshiped and worried over. Some say it liberates men; others, that it enslaves them. People can get very emotional about the subject of money, especially when there is either very much or very little of it. One way or another, money matters—to most people, it matters a great deal.

The reason the subject of money almost invariably arises in a discussion of achievement is that the two so frequently go hand in hand—not always, but often. There are, of course, some types of success that have nothing whatever to do with money; but there are many others in which financial rewards follow great achievements, and the promise of those rewards sometimes inspires those achievements to begin with. For the very ambitious Christian, the implications of seeking and making large amounts of money often are more than abstractions. Moneymaking is an issue about which he hears contradictory opinions and one that he ultimately must sort out for himself.

What does scripture say about money?

A good place to start is to point out some things scripture does *not* say about money.

First, the Bible does *not* say that money is either bad or good.

That would seem rather obvious, but there are those in the church who regard money itself as being somehow intrinsically evil, with special powers to corrupt that are so irresistible that a Christian cannot wisely have anything at all to do with it. A surprisingly large number of Christians misread the often-quoted verse 1 Timothy 6:10 to say that money is the root of all evil and take that point of departure to regard money as an evil thing in and of itself.

The Bible does not teach this, of course. Money is like any other material object or commodity: In and of itself, it is neither good nor bad. It is a tool, a vehicle. It can be used for both good and evil things, and it is the use to which it is put and the attitude we have toward it that make it a curse or a blessing. Like fire, it can either warm the house or destroy it. Money is neither sinful nor sacred. It is just there.

A balanced reading of scripture shows this approach to money. There are hundreds of references to money in the Bible, ranging from instructions on giving to matter-of-fact descriptions of certain financial exchanges between characters in the various narratives. Scripture certainly does speak to the issue of money, but never with the shrill illogic of some of today's Christians. It treats it as a fact of life that is to be handled responsibly by the Christian, not as a thing to be either worshiped or shunned.

A second thing the Bible does *not* say about money is this: It does not say that poverty is a virtue.

It intrigues me that so many people applaud the spiritual advantages of poverty, while declining to participate voluntarily in the experience. Christ certainly had special compassion for the poor, just as He did for underdogs and the disenfranchised of every type. Christ, like the father who helps the smallest of his children cross the street, always looked to help those with the greatest need. He lived in a day, like ours, of great economic disparity; and His heart went out to the have-nots. He grieved over their condition and became angry when people with more financial and social clout abused or humiliated them. But it is a mistake to interpret His concern for them as indicating that He loved them more because they were down-and-outers or that He regarded their poverty as a spiritually uplifting condition.

Poverty has been rather heavily romanticized in our wealthy Western culture. It is popular to talk of the lessons it teaches, the humility it inspires, the strength of character it produces. That view is, unfortunately, a myth of the middle class. It certainly is not shared by the poor themselves. There is as much meanness of spirit, as much spiritual emptiness, even as much pride, in one economic level as in any other. To feel that there is something particularly ennobling about financial insecurity unfortunately ignores most of the evidence on the subject.

A third misconception of what the Bible says about money—and a sharply contrasting one—is particularly popular in recent years. It is the concept that good Christians will always be prosperous, that it is God's will for all His children to be financially well fixed. As attractive as the idea is, it also falls into a category of middle-class myth.

Those who hold this notion usually cite 3 John 2: "Beloved, I wish above all things that thou mayest prosper and be in health, even as thy soul prospereth." God wants the best for His children, the argument goes, and those who are truly in His will can count on having the best of everything, which presumably includes a big house, big car, big bank account, the whole package. The logical conclusion is that people who have less than that are either not operating consistently enough within God's will or else have simply not "claimed" all these material blessings with an adequate exercise of faith.

Like the poor-is-better theory, this viewpoint overlooks the available evidence in scripture, which shows that people of various financial conditions are to be found in the center of God's approval.

> There are the rich and the poor
>   the sick and healthy
>   people of high and low social class
>   servants and masters

each one of them, in his own setting, responding to God in his own individual way, drawing from his own experiences the lessons God wants him to learn from life.

The argument that God, since He wants the best for His children, must want them to be wealthy betrays a wholly secular view of what "the best" is. The best thing for us may not necessarily be the most expensive or the most comfortable item. God does want the best for us, but we must let Him—and not Madison Avenue—define *best* in each particular case. If the Bible is clear on anything at all, it clearly teaches that God's way of measuring worth is sometimes different from man's. We cannot impose our own definition of *the best* on Him.

It is God's will that His children should prosper, but prosperity is not always synonymous with material plenty. When we assume that prosperity in the biblical sense will include upper-middle-class luxuries, we are moving beyond what the Bible promises. We may indeed acquire those things, but we are not guaranteed them, and we cannot assume that they indicate God's blanket approval of us if they come. Nor can we strike postures of spiritual superiority over our Christian brother who is still struggling to pay the bills. Offer him a job, yes. Pray for him, yes. But do not assume that his growth is somehow spiritually stunted, and that if he will do so, he can simply pray his way out of debt. It does not always work out that way.

There is an impressive diversity of people in God's Kingdom. It was true in Bible days, and it is true today. At a chapel service at Lee College, recently, a colleague of mine announced that his sermon topic would be "How I Found God With a Nine-Iron." I started to turn him off immediately. *A nine-iron indeed!* I thought. *How can one find God with a nine-iron?* (I've never found anything with a nine-iron but pain and agony—and a few hundred sand traps.) But by the time the speaker had finished speaking, I agreed that he *had* in fact found God with a nine-iron, in a most peculiar and personal way that could have happened only to him.

The lesson I learned that day was never to underestimate the diverse ways in which people experience the Kingdom. If God teaches some people with nine-irons, surely He might teach others lessons at the unemployment office or at the Mercedes dealership, through material wealth or through lack of it. As tantalizing as it is to believe that His blessings to us will always include financial prosperity, we simply cannot conclude that from scripture.

11

What Does the Bible Say About Money?

If these are misconceptions of what the scripture says regarding money, what *does* the Bible teach?

Consider these:

1. *Hard work for financial gain is expected of us and not to be discouraged.*

The Book of Proverbs contains many expressions of this principle:

> All hard work brings a profit, but mere talk leads only to poverty.
>
> Proverbs 14:23 NIV

> The plans of the diligent lead to profit as surely as haste leads to poverty.
>
> Proverbs 21:5 NIV

> Lazy hands make a man poor, but diligent hands bring wealth.
>
> Proverbs 10:4 NIV

Nor are such examples limited to the Old Testament. In Romans 12:11, Paul challenges the Christians of the early church not to be "slothful in business," referring in this case to all the affairs of the church. In another passage, he tells the church straightforwardly that the unproductive should not eat:

For even when we were with you, this we com-
manded you, that if any would not work, neither
should he eat.

2 Thessalonians 3:10

This is consistent with Paul's own example. He personally
worked as a tentmaker, even while intensely involved in his
missionary ministry, in order to keep the bills paid. He apparently did not regard such profit-seeking behavior as unwor-
thy or as a thing that compromised his status as an apostle.
He did it because it needed to be done, because the money
had to be made to keep the people and the work of the church
going.

Keep in mind that this is the same man who gave us that
thrilling promise of God's provision: "But my God shall supply all your need according to his riches in glory by Christ
Jesus." He obviously believed that promise to be true and lived
by it. But he did not sit around idly waiting for God to supply.
He apparently understood that, in some situations, the way
God supplies our needs is by giving us an opportunity to work
hard to earn the things we need.

Cynics have said of God's people that they are too heavenly
minded to be of any earthly good. That could certainly not be
said of Paul. He never disparaged hard work, even of a secular
sort, to finance the work of the Kingdom.

Nor should we. While one member of the body preaches in
the marketplace, another must keep things going at the tent
factory! When one Christian takes the Gospel to the far cor-
ners of the earth, another must stay home to pay the air fare.
The Kingdom needs honest, hardworking members, busily
making money at secular enterprises, to keep the wheels of
ministry turning. It is ironic that some of the contemporary
ministries that most emphasize the "simple life" and rail at the
evils of materialism in suburban congregations rarely miss a
chance to solicit dollars from those congregations.

2. *God is not as much concerned with how much money we have as with our attitude toward it.*

The irascible Mark Twain once muttered: "I'm opposed to millionaires as a matter of principle . . . but it would be dangerous to offer me the position!" That distrust of the wealthy has always existed among the not-so-wealthy, especially in the church. Okay, we say, maybe God doesn't mind if a person is comfortable, but to actually be *rich* surely must be discouraged in the Bible.

On the contrary, the Bible seems not nearly so concerned with how much money one has—even if it is a very large amount—as with one's attitude toward it. The Bible tells of very wealthy men who walked closely with God, such as David, Abraham, Job. Not only did He not take their money away from them, but in Job's case He restored his wealth to him—with a 100 percent long-term capital gain!—after Satan had taken it away. In Deuteronomy 8:18, the Bible talks about God giving power to acquire wealth. Proverbs 3:9, 10 similarly offers a formula for having material abundance.

The key is one's attitude toward wealth, not the acquiring of wealth itself. To the person who depends on his wealth to guarantee happiness, rather than depending on the Lord, it is a source of sin, and ultimately of sorrow.

> Whoever trusts in his riches will fall, but the righteous will thrive like a green leaf.
>
> Proverbs 11:28 NIV

The tendency to have a false sense of security in riches is perhaps the single greatest danger of wealth. The strongest warning of this hazard is in Paul's first letter to Timothy:

> Tell those who are rich in this present world not to be contemptuous of others, and not to rest the weight of their confidence on the transitory power of wealth but on the living God, who generously gives us

everything for our enjoyment. Tell them to do good, to be rich in kindly actions, to be ready to give to others and to sympathise with those in distress. Their security should be invested in the life to come, so that they may be sure of holding a share in the life which is real and permanent.

1 Timothy 6:17–19 PHILLIPS

This verse goes to the heart of the question of wealth for a Christian. It is, first, a clear statement that persons may be both wealthy and Christian—else why the need for this instruction? It is, second, a warning to the wealthy to hold proper attitudes toward their wealth, particularly not to trust their lives to their money. And, third, it points out some of the other specific attitudes of the rich that are unchristian—such as contempt for the poor and lack of generosity to others.

That single verse contains an outline of all one needs to know about wealth in the life of a Christian.

The Bible certainly issues many warnings about the deceitfulness of riches, the potential of great wealth to lure people away from simple faith in God, and the problems that occur when the rich behave arrogantly toward the poor. The caution lights are there in the Bible, and any Christian who is financially well fixed, even if he doesn't regard himself as "rich," would be foolish to brush them lightly aside. Warnings that occur as frequently as these cannot be easily disregarded.

The balance of scripture (Old Testament as well as New), however, clearly does not teach that the acquisition of wealth is a condition that disqualifies a person from a close, spiritually sensitive walk with God.

3. *Christians who are financially prosperous have a responsibility to be generous to other people and to the work of the Kingdom of God.*

It is axiomatic that every blessing brings with it responsibility, and that is true of material gain for the Christian.

Throughout biblical history—from the tithing system of the Old Testament to the communal giving in the early church—there was always a requirement that the people of God give back to Him a portion of their money. Those with adequate money for their own needs are told to be generous to the poor as well as to support the work of the church.

The willingness of believers to give generously to God is even linked to one's own prosperity, in Proverbs 3:9 (NIV):

> Honor the Lord with your wealth, with the first-fruits of all your crops.

In discussions of giving, as well as in other financial matters, the focus of scripture is once again on the attitude of the individual rather than on the amount of money involved. Remember the story of the woman who anointed Jesus with expensive perfume?

> Jesus himself was now in Bethany in the house of Simon the leper. As he was sitting at table, a woman approached him with an alabaster flask of very costly spikenard perfume. She broke the neck of the flask and poured the perfume on Jesus' head. Some of those present were highly indignant and muttered,
> "What is the point of such wicked waste of perfume? It could have been sold for over thirty pounds and the money given to the poor." And there was a murmur of resentment against her. But Jesus said,
> "Let her alone, why must you make her feel uncomfortable? She has done a beautiful thing for me. You have the poor with you always and you can do good to them whenever you like, but you will not always have me."
>
> Mark 14:3–7 PHILLIPS

Here we see an example of Jesus shifting attention from the cost of the woman's offering to the spirit in which it was given.

The disciples on that occasion were upset by the price tag; Jesus was more interested in the woman's heart.

In another familiar story, Jesus praised a widow who gave a small offering as an act of worship to God. The amount was insignificant; but Jesus, once again, called attention not to the amount, but to the generous spirit the woman had. We are entirely too attentive to the bottom line, even in the things of God. We are too often more concerned with who *gives* how much, who *has* how much, who is richer or poorer than whom. Our attention is diverted from our responsibility to love others regardless of their net-worth statements and to look past their financial statements to see their hearts. That was the pattern Christ set.

The matter of giving to the Lord becomes, then, a personal matter that is resolved in the heart of each believer. But the Christian with plenty must face his responsibility to give plenty—not because men are watching and not because God will zap him if he doesn't, but because generosity of spirit is one of the vital signs of the Christian walk. If having material goods involves additional challenges in the Christ-like life—and it does—the prosperous Christian must be even more careful than others to observe all such indicators of spiritual health.

The church needs Christians who make large amounts of money. It may sound terribly unspiritual to say so, but it is the simple truth that the work of the Kingdom is very expensive work. In sheer dollars and cents, it takes a lot of fuel to keep the physical apparatus operating. The people responsible for almost every major ministry in the Christian world will acknowledge that their fund-raising efforts would be severely hampered if, for some reason, they could receive contributions only from those Christians making less than $10,000 a year. There are scores of worthy ministries, and they need the financial support of tens of thousands of prosperous Christians. For that to happen, the Christian must not only be willing to give it, but must have it to give. Either one without the other will not get the job done.

The church must encourage its people to work hard, manage wisely, and keep the purse strings available to God's touch. There is no room in that relationship for harsh, angry denunciations of wealth and profit, and the prosperous Christian must not be intimidated by that attitude when he encounters it. Like the widow and her mite, it ultimately comes down to an affair of the heart; and the prosperous Christian, no less than the poor one, can confidently trust the motives of his own heart as a reliable guide.

4. *Whenever material things gain a higher priority than spiritual ones, the system is out of balance.*

Money matters are essentially matters of balance. There can be few rigid rules. Anyone who attempts to make a comprehensive formula for the individual Christian and his money runs the risk of running afoul of this or that biblical precedent. It is an area calling for a high degree of individual decision making.

There are a few questions that one can ask himself to help monitor his own priorities regarding material things:

Am I so involved in the pursuit of material things that I no longer actively pursue God?

Have I become so accustomed to working for large amounts of money that I have become unwilling to work for the Kingdom without pay?

Are my financial obligations so great that I would be unable to follow God to a new setting if He specifically led me, by His Spirit, to make a change?

Have I gained such admiration for those who are able to make lots of money that I can no longer have admiration for those whose achievements are in not-so-lucrative areas?

And perhaps the most revealing question of all, and the most difficult to answer:

> Do I enjoy the material comforts so much that I would be unwilling to give them up, should God call on me to do so?

That last question will probably never be asked, except as a hypothetical exercise. There are few conceivable situations in which a Christian might be called upon to give up material prosperity to prove his love for God. But the question is still a good private barometer, because it goes straight to the heart of one's priorities. It asks, in effect, whom we serve, God or mammon? To the typical comfortable, successful middle-class Christian who asks it honestly, it can be a troubling question, because none of us wishes to give up the things we have acquired. We worked for them. We earned them. We deserve to have them.

But that is exactly what Jesus asked the wealthy young man in Mark 10:17–22 (PHILLIPS).

> As he began to take the road again, a man came running up and fell at his feet, and asked him,
> "Good master, tell me, please, what must I do to be sure of eternal life?"
> "Why do you call me good?" returned Jesus. "No one is good—only God. You know the commandments, 'Do no murder, Do not commit adultery, Do not steal, Do not bear false witness, Do not cheat, Honour thy father and mother'."
> "Master," he replied, "I have carefully kept all these since I was quite young."
> Jesus looked steadily at him, and his heart warmed towards him. Then he said,
> "There is one thing you still need. Go and sell

everything you have, give the money away to the poor—you will have riches in Heaven. And then come back and follow me."

At these words his face fell and he went away in deep distress, for he was very rich.

It was the ultimate spiritual challenge, and the young man flunked it. Why? Not because he was rich or even because Jesus wanted him to give his money away. Some have interpreted the story that way, but I believe this story has nothing to do with money. It has to do with self-definition. Jesus didn't want the man's money; He could have created money for the poor, out of thin air, if He had really been interested in the money.

What He wanted was for the young man to *define himself* in terms of the Kingdom—to say, by his actions, that his money was not as important to him as the Kingdom of God. "What is your top priority?" He was asking the young man. "Is it your money, or is it the Kingdom?" And that was the point at which he failed to measure up. I personally believe that if the man had agreed to sell everything and give the money away, Jesus would have told him it was unnecessary, and we would perhaps never have heard the story at all. But the man, when forced to look closely at himself, admitted that, in his scheme of things, the Kingdom had second priority.

God can be happy for us to be wealthy, if we can be happy *not* to be.

Does God want to keep us at the subsistence level, in order to keep our hearts pure before Him? Of course not. He wishes good things for us, including material things, but He wants us to be involved enough with Him that we know how to live either way.

As usual, the Apostle Paul says it best: "I know how to live when things are difficult and I know how to live when things are prosperous. In general and in particular I have learned the secret . . . of facing *either* plenty or poverty. I am ready for anything through the strength of the One who lives within me" (Philippians 4:12 PHILLIPS).

12
The Positive Thought Life

Positive thinking didn't begin with Norman Vincent Peale. It began long before there were names like Napoleon Hill

or Robert Schuller
or Clement Stone
or Wayne Dyer
or Jonathan Livingston Seagull

or books like *The Magic of Thinking Big* or catchphrases like "positive mental attitude" or seminars on building a healthy self-concept.

Long before positive thinking became an international movement, it was a teaching of scripture.

"As a man thinks," the Bible says, "so is he." It cannot be put more simply than that.

The most critical factors in one's life are his attitude, his mental posture, and his way of thinking about himself and the people around him. There is power in the positive thought life. There always has been, and there always will be. Sometimes Christians, unlikely as it seems, are the first to forget that. Some Christians have so strongly associated positive-thinking concepts with commercial ventures and salesmanship that they dismiss those concepts as just another part of a secular, materialistic approach to life.

"I get tired of hearing about this positive-thinking stuff all the time," a minister once said to me. "We need to forget all that and just get back to the basics."

The basics? What could be more basic than a person's willingness to think good thoughts? What could be more basic than one's mental life, than the environment inside one's head? As we think, the Bible says, so *are* we! What could possibly be more basic than that?

God has known from before the Creation what man is just learning: that the most important space in the world is that small space between our ears. What goes on there will determine the degree to which we succeed or fail at almost everything we do. What goes on there will determine whether we are happy or unhappy, regardless of the situations we find ourselves in. It will decide whether we are victors or victims in life.

We *are* what we *think,* and we can control what we think.

If we could do nothing to control what goes on in that mental space of ours, it would do little good to talk of the power of positive thought. But we can fill our minds with whatever we choose; we can decide what goes on there.

The Bible spells it out: "Whatsoever things are true,

> whatsoever things are honest,
> whatsoever things are just,
> whatsoever things are pure,
> whatsoever things are lovely,
> whatsoever things are of good report;
>> if there be any virtue, and if there be any praise, think
>> on these things" (Philippians 4:8) .

God would not challenge us to "think on these things" if we had no control over our thoughts. That scripture is a clear signal that we can have whatever thought life we choose. "Fill all your thoughts with these things," is the way another translation expresses it. *"Fix* your minds" on good things, says another version of the same verse. In every rendering the message is emphatic: The Christian has control over his own mental space, and he is to fill that space with positive thoughts. In the arena of our own minds, we make it happen; we choose what is there!

It is on that firm scriptural ground that we approach every new day with confidence and optimism. The principles of positive thinking are more than just the motivator's hype, more than so much pep rally razzle-dazzle. We do indeed have the power to change the world we live in by changing the world inside our own minds. We have that ability to take control. God gave it to us. He challenges us to use it.

We are, after all, His children. We are the sons and daughters of a God who wants good things for us. And so with that confidence, in that faith, we fill our minds with

positive expectations
lofty ambitions
high goals

and we constantly work to make those things happen!